Endorsements

"Caswell's work on Thomas Patient gives vital insight on the relationship of the early Particular Baptists to one another, their theological vitality, their church planting energy, and their willingness to suffer for what they believed to be clearly revealed truth. The careful development of the practice and theology of believers' baptism by immersion also is discussed with clarity and contextual relevance in a comparison of the work of Norcott with that of Patient. How the life and thought of Patient is relevant for contemporary discussions of Baptist identity is also addressed in a clear and informative way. This book makes the fabric of early Baptist historiography a more tightly woven garment."

—**Tom Nettles,** Senior Professor of Historical Theology, The Southern Baptist Theological Seminary, Louisville, KY

"Far too many of us automatically assume that being Irish means being Roman Catholic. That is neither true today nor has it been so in the past. Thomas Patient's transatlantic story is a good case in point. His most important ministry as a Particular Baptist lay in Ireland where he was instrumental in laying the foundations for the Irish Baptist community, which has had an especially significant history in the north of Ireland. Moreover, Caswell does not think that the rich details of Patient's ministry are of mere antiquarian interest, since he is rightly convinced that such a life has much to teach us today."

—**Michael A.G. Haykin,** Chair and Professor of Church History, The Southern Baptist Theological Seminary, Louisville, KY

"Whether we realize it or not, we derive much of our identity from our family—the legacy of those who have gone before us. This holds true when it comes to our church family. In a word, we owe a great deal to many whom we have never met. In the present volume, Micah Caswell introduces us to one long-forgotten family member by the name of Thomas Patient, whose pioneer work in Ireland was pivotal to the establishment of Baptist churches and the spread of Baptist ideals in the early seventeenth century. As the reader will discover, Patient's endurance in suffering, faithfulness in preaching, and commitment to Christ, make him a family member worthy of admiration and imitation."

—**J. Stephen Yuille,** Vice President of Academics and Academic Dean of College, Heritage College & Seminary, Cambridge, ON; Associate Professor of Biblical Spirituality, The Southern Baptist Theological Seminary, Louisville, KY

"Far too often we are quick to forget those who came before us. Micah Caswell shines an important light on the life and work of Thomas Patient; an almost forgotten Baptist father who suffered much for the faith, wrote one of the earliest English works on believer's baptism and helped strengthen the Baptist movement in England, North America, and especially Ireland."

—**Joshua Stone,** Pastor, Fellowship Baptist Church, Parry Sound, ON

"It's been said that the best of men are just men at best. That's partially true. Men are men, but Christian men should stand at the forefront. Christian men should be men of conviction, courage, and boldness fueled by a biblical worldview for all of life. In his book, *Thomas Patient: The Father of the Irish Baptist Church*, Micah Caswell writes about a Christian man shaped, formed, and fueled by a biblical worldview for the glory of God. Whether you've heard of Thomas Patient or not, you will benefit from this book about a man whose life was marked by love for Jesus, the Church, and the people of God. May the Lord raise many more men like Thomas Patient in our day, for the glory of Christ, the spread of the gospel, and the building up of local churches."

—**Dave Jenkins,** Executive Director, Servants of Grace Ministries; Executive Editor, *Theology for Life Magazine*; Host, Equipping You in Grace Podcast

"Sometimes the best way to recover our theological moorings is to go back into church history and examine the lives of those who have gone before us. Micah Caswell's work on Thomas Patient, who established the first Irish Baptist Church in days of political and ecclesiological turmoil in the seventeenth century, enables us to do just that. This little known story of a faithful Christian minister with Baptist convictions will encourage and challenge all who continue to contend for the gospel today."

—**Kirk Wellum,** Principal and Professor of Systematic Theology and Pastoral Studies, Toronto Baptist Seminary and Bible College, Toronto, ON

"Caswell's ground-breaking look at Thomas Patient provides crucial context on the development of early Baptists, both theologically, politically, and socially. The fascinating connection that Patient had with pivotal moments in history, from the English Civil War to the signing of the *1644 London Baptist Confession*, is set alongside his own personal zeal for church planting and Baptist ecclesiology. Caswell also reveals the trials that the non-conformist Patient faced, from trans-Atlantic journeys, to internal denominational strife, to long imprisonments. This new look into the life of a great, if flawed, Baptist leader will provide valuable resources for scholars and practical encouragement for Christians."

—**Matthew Lyon,** (PhD in Baptist History, The Southern Baptist Theological Seminary) Pastor, Chesapeake Baptist Church, Severn, MD; Host, History and Hope Podcast.

Thomas Patient:
The Father of the Irish Baptist Church

Micah L. Caswell

THOMAS PATIENT

The Father of the Irish Baptist Church

Foreword by MALCOLM B. YARNELL III

Thomas Patient: The Father of the Irish Baptist Church

Copyright © 2019 by Micah L. Caswell
Published by: H&E Publishing, Peterborough, Canada
www.hesedandemet.com
Cover design: Kseniia Piddubna

All rights reserved. This book or any portion thereof may not be reproduced or used in any manner whatsoever without the express written permission of the publisher except for the use of brief quotations in a book review.

First Edition, 2019

Paperback ISBN: 978-1-989174-28-9
eBook ISBN: 978-1-989174-41-8

Acknowledgements

Thomas Patient traveled a good but difficult road. Gospel convictions can lead to trials and he had his share; always at Thomas' side however, was his faithful wife Sarah. I frequently thought of Sarah as I studied Thomas, and it reminded me of Proverbs 18:22 which says, "He who finds a wife finds a good thing and obtains favor from the Lord." Being a pastor's wife is a difficult calling and takes a woman of unique grace and grit. Like Thomas Patient, I have found a good wife to travel alongside me through the twists and turns of life and ministry. Kristen has been an oasis for me the past fifteen years. As we have raised two children, planted four churches, survived a church split, completed four graduate degrees, lived in three cities, and transformed seven houses into homes, I find I love my life more because Kristen is by my side. The Lord has indeed shown me great favor by blessing me with my lovely bride. He has also blessed me with two wonderful children, Mason Lawrence and Kenlee Grace.

I would like to acknowledge and thank Dr. Michael A.G. Haykin. He served as my advisor and main reader at Toronto Baptist Seminary. Without his guidance and care this work would have never become a reality. Due to pastoral commitments, this was an unusually slow project to develop. However, Dr. Haykin graciously remained an open door and encouraged me all along the way. He took on the burden of giving me his time as well as lovingly critiquing me when needed. I am honored to consider him a mentor and a friend. Dr. Haykin is someone I deeply admire and it has been a great joy to get to work with him and be in his orbit.

Thank you Dr. Barry Howson of Heritage College and Seminary, who served as my second reader at TBS and provided helpful feedback that greatly improved the book.

Thank you Dr. Malcolm B. Yarnell III for contributing the foreword. I was honored by your contribution. Traveling to Regent's Park, Oxford with you was the highlight of my time at Southwestern Baptist Theological Seminary. It was with you in Oxford that I fell in love with Baptist history. You were also the one who put together the pieces of my Baptist ecclesiology which has then informed my pastoral ministry. Brother, I am forever grateful.

I would like to thank the staff at Toronto Baptist Seminary who helped get this project across the finish line. Thank you, Kirk Wellum for giving extra time to the project and being such an encouragement.

Thank you also to Dr. Larry Kreitzer of Regent's Park, Oxford for providing insights into Thomas Patient's relationship to William Kiffen. Thank you, Emily Burgoyne and the staff at the Angus Library at Regent's Park, Oxford for assisting in my research.

Finally, I would like to thank Chance Faulkner and his team at H&E Publishing. It has been a delight to work with H&E. I am excited about the future of H&E under Chance's leadership.

Thomas Patient displayed courageous and pioneering gospel convictions. I marvel at all that God accomplished through him. Modern church planters display similar courageous convictions and I want to acknowledge all the ordinary church planters of the Southern Baptist Convention and Acts 29 Network. You are my heroes.

About the Author

Micah is married to Kristen and they have two children. He grew up in Denton, Texas and graduated from the University of North Texas. He also holds degrees from Dallas Seminary, Southwestern Baptist Seminary, Toronto Baptist Seminary, and holds his doctorate from The Southern Baptist Theological Seminary. He has pastored at churches in Austin and Houston. Micah is the pastor of Redeemer Church in Denton, Texas which he planted in 2013.

CONTENTS

THE IMPORTANCE OF THE IRISH BAPTISTS xv
Malcolm B. Yarnell III

THOMAS PATIENT

PREFACE xxiii
INTRODUCTION xxv
1. EARLY LIFE & MINISTRY 1
2. IRISH MINISTRY 25
3. DUBLIN MINISTRY 39
4. *ON BAPTISM* 51
CONCLUSION 101
APPENDIX: A LETTER FROM WATERFORD 129
BIBLIOGRAPHY 133
SUBJECT INDEX 139
SCRIPTURE INDEX 145

The Importance of the Irish Baptists

Malcolm B. Yarnell III

Rehearsing the lives of believers who have been graced with faithful lives is one of the most edifying Christian activities available. For example, the Apostle Paul sometimes pointed to an exemplary life and thanked God for the joy that person of integrity generated in his own heart. If Paul could laud both Timothy and Epaphroditus in Philippians 2, then Micah Caswell may lift up Thomas Patient (d. 1666), whom he entitles, "The Father of the Irish Baptist Church." While Patient's early years are shrouded in mystery, the final decades of his life intensely reflect God's glory. The first Irish Baptist church leader sought to fully obey the Lord's will, and his example will inspire you toward faithfulness.

Patient's story is worth remembering not only because he was faithful to pursue truth through great difficulty, but also because he introduces us to the importance of the Irish Baptists. Denominational presentations of Baptist life have typically centered on England before proceeding toward a fulsome consideration of American developments and worldwide growth thereafter. Alas, our histories too often fail to emphasize the importance of the Irish connection (although the Welsh and Scottish connections are more well-known). The critical contribution of the Irish Baptist connection began to leap out at me during my own research into the life of Christopher Blackwood (1605–1670), who was known to the Cromwells as "The Oracle of the Anabaptists in Ireland."[1] Later, while looking into the origins of the Salters' Hall debate over the Trinity, it became evident that the Particular Baptist defense of classical orthodoxy actually began with an Irish Baptist physician vigorously pursuing the prosecution of a heretical Dissenter, Thomas Emlyn (1663–1741).[2] However, the demonstrable importance of Ireland to the Baptist cause now leaps forward with a huge bound through the publication of this book.

Caswell buttresses the evidence that Ireland was influential upon Baptist developments by chronicling the life and theology of Thomas Patient. Patient came to his Baptist convictions, Caswell reminds us, while pursuing the biblical truth about baptism among the early Puritans of America. After converting to Baptist views, he became a co-signatory of the *First London Baptist Confession* in 1644 and published an early defense of the baptismal ordinance. Subsequently, two of the greatest early English Particular Baptists, William Kiffen and

---

[1] Malcolm B. Yarnell III, "Christopher Blackwood (1605–1670)," in *The Particular Baptist: A Series of Biographical Essays on Notable Figures*, ed. Michael A.G. Haykin and Terry Wolever, Revised ed. (Springfield, MO: Particular Baptist Press, 2019), 1:117–150.

[2] Malcolm B. Yarnell III, "'The Point in Question' at Salters' Hall: Baptists Contending for Trinity, Scripture, and Freedom," in *Trinity, Creed, and Confusion: The Salters' Hall Debates of 1719*, ed. Stephen Copson (Oxford, England: Centre for Baptist History and Heritage, forthcoming 2019). Cf. Malcolm B. Yarnell III, "Baptists and Classical Trinitarianism," in *Baptists and the Christian Tradition*, ed. Matthew Y. Emerson, Christopher W. Morgan, and R. Lucas Stamps (Nashville: B&H Academic, forthcoming 2020); idem, *God the Trinity: Biblical Portraits* (Nashville, TN: B&H Academic, 2016).

The Importance of the Irish Baptists

Hanserd Knollys, laid hands upon Patient. The connection between Kiffen and Patient proved particularly helpful in keeping Baptists from joining the failed Fifth Monarchists. The local presence of Patient in Ireland alongside the distant authority of Kiffen in London was enough to persuade the Irish Baptists away from following the siren song of eschatological enthusiasm.

Patient established the first Baptist church in Ireland in the 1650s and built the first Baptist chapel in 1653 in Swift's Alley, Dublin. That congregation continues its existence today. Patient engaged in his church-planting ministry while serving as a chaplain in the English army. Patient's example establishes the truth, Caswell argues, that religious liberty was not necessarily the central Baptist distinctive it has sometimes been presented to be. Rather than the liberty of conscience and the separation of church and state, which are certainly important to most Baptists, Patient focused upon regenerate church membership and the baptism of believers by immersion. Patient also exemplifies the importance of covenant theology among the early Particular Baptists, although his Baptist version of covenant theology necessarily differed from the Reformed construal. After his Irish sojourn, the Baptist leader suffered imprisonment in Bristol, but he then ended his days as an honored leader of the influential Particular Baptist congregation in Devonshire Square, London.

While one need not agree entirely with the theology of Patient, as Caswell himself demonstrates, one certainly must agree that the Irish contribution to the Baptist movement had a profound beginning with Thomas Patient. Moreover, one must certainly agree that the Irish Baptist movement requires further consideration within the Baptist academy. Showcasing the importance of Thomas Patient in Ireland, as in England and America—where he defended and suffered for the biblical truths of personal regeneration by the sovereign God and the immersion of believers alone by the church—should spur further research into this significant branch of the Baptist family of churches. Micah Caswell is to be commended, not only for writing an interesting story of an interesting life, but for reminding us of the importance of the Irish for the Baptists.

    Malcolm B. Yarnell III
    Texas
    August 15, 2019

Chronology

1591
Birth

1638
The foundation of the first Particular Baptist Church in London

1642–1646
First stage of the English Civil War

late 1630s–1643
In the American colonies

1643
Begins serving with William Kiffen in London

1643–1644
Evangelistic tour in Kent

1644
Signed *First London Confession of Faith*

1648–1651
Second stage of the English Civil War

1650
Serves in Ireland as an Army chaplain

1650
Founds Irish Baptist Church in Waterford

1651–1660
Commonwealth period largely marked by Cromwell ruling as Lord Protectorate

1651
Founds Irish Baptist Church in Dublin including erecting the first Baptist church structure in Ireland

1654
Publishes *On Baptism*

1660–1664
Returns to England to serve the Pithay Baptist Church in Bristol

1663
Arrested for violations of the Clarendon Code's Act of Uniformity & Conventicle Act

1664–1666
Serves as an Elder in William Kiffen's church in London

1666
Death during the plague

1669
Death of Sarah Patient

Preface

Baptists need to know their identity. For generations Baptists have asked, "What does it mean to be a Baptist?" Studying the life of Thomas Patient is certainly encouraging to all Christians today because it gives us a glimpse into a faithful life. His life was also pioneering and thus very fascinating. However, exploring Patient's life is also helpful for Baptists to discover their identity. He certainly endured in running the race set before him (Hebrews 12:1). He faithfully ran from England, to the American colonies, back to England, then onto Ireland to establish the Baptist movement in a new land. Related, his spiritual journey developed from English Puritan, to an American Baptist, to an English Particular Baptist, to founding the first Irish Baptist churches. Thomas Patient ran quite a race. In the end, readers will see a shining example of how to live faithful to the Bible. Further, Patient teaches modern Baptists that our identity has less to do with the concept of soul competency and more to do with applying the biblical doctrine of believer's baptism by immersion.

Introduction

Thomas Patient lived during a fascinating and significant period of British history and played a leading role in an emerging and lasting religious movement. Today the largest Protestant denomination in America, the Southern Baptist Convention, can trace their roots to the British Calvinistic Baptists who were part of the English Reformation's Puritan movement. Thomas Patient was a significant figure in that initial movement. During his life, he journeyed from England to America, back to England, and later to Ireland. He was one of 15 men who signed the *First London Confession* in 1644 as the assistant pastor to William Kiffen at his church in London. Patient was also one of two key Baptist leaders during the Cromwellian occupation of Ireland in the 1650s. During his ministry in Ireland, he published *On Baptism*, led the influential Christ Church in Dublin, and built the first Baptist structure in Ireland. Michael Haykin notes Kiffen's "earnest desire to follow the Scriptures whatever the cost."[1] What was true of William Kiffen was also

---

[1] Michael A.G. Haykin, *Kiffen, Knollys and Keach: Rediscovering Our English Baptist Heritage* (Peterborough, Canada: H&E Publishing, 2019), 52. One can easily argue that the Baptist ecclesiological experiment is an attempt at exclusive or at least primary biblical authority. Haykin supports his claim by citing a compliment that Kiffen

true of Thomas Patient. His commitment to the Bible led him to a Calvinistic soteriology, a Baptistic ecclesiology, and a missionary zeal for church planting. These biblical commitments and values remain in the modern Baptist movement.

In what follows, the author has sought to delineate the significance of Thomas Patient to the story of the seventeenth-century Baptists, especially with regard to their theology. His geographical and theological journey will be traced from English Puritan to American Baptist to English Particular Baptist to Irish army chaplain and church planter. The path of his life and theology will give useful evidence to the continuing conversation over Baptist identity. Patient's life highlights that early Baptists were committed to the Bible's authority in their theology including the doctrines of ecclesiology and believer's baptism, and that they were committed to partnering together to spread the gospel. Readers will also see that the theology of religious liberty was not an original Baptist distinctive but was developed later in America.

---

paid John Norcott (1621-1676) which is cited in Joseph Ivimey's *A History of the English Baptists* (London: B. J. Holdsworth, 1823), III, 300. Kiffen said, "He steered his whole course by the compass of the word, making Scripture precept or example his constant rule in matters of religion. Other men's opinions or interpretations were not the standard by which he went; but, through the assistance of the Holy Spirit, he laboured to find out what the Lord himself had said in his word." This was Kiffen's compliment of Norcott, but obviously also a standard he sought for himself.

1
Early Life & Ministry

Early Life

Thomas Patient opens his introductory comments of *On Baptism* by referencing John 9:4. His life is evidence that he genuinely desired to fervently "run that Christian race"[1] set before him because "the night cometh when no man can work."[2] His race led him from England to the New England colonies, back to England, then to Ireland, then back to England where he died during the Great Plague in 1666.[3] Patient made his mark despite the fact that his Baptist contemporaries Kiffen, Knollys, and Blackwood outlived him. Gribben correctly comments that much of his life is "shrouded in mystery" but

---

[1] Thomas Patient, *On the Doctrine of Baptism, And the Distinction of the Covenants* (London: Henry Hills, 1654), 2.

[2] Patient, *On the Doctrine*, 2.

[3] The National Archives reports, "This was the worst outbreak of plague in England since the black death of 1348. London lost roughly 15% of its population. While 68,596 deaths were recorded in the city, the true number was probably over 100,000." http://www.nationalarchives.gov.uk/education/lesson49.htm (accessed on April 1, 2013).

enough evidence remains to see a man committed to "God's glory and the service of his generation."[4]

The most significant biographical information on Patient is his own personal account found in the "Epistle to the Christian Reader," his preface to *On the Doctrine of Baptism*. He was possibly born in 1591,[5] but there are conflicting reports regarding this date. Little is known of his professional pursuits before his pastoral ministry. James Ware claims that Patient was a "Bodicemaker or Tailor by Trade."[6] Nothing is known of Patient's family background or his upbringing, but he was certainly a Puritan by the 1630s, which undoubtedly drove him to the New England colonies.[7] Crosby classifies him as an Independent minister in New England.[8] The likelihood that Patient was initially an Independent is highly probable because many other Independents (Congregationalists) went to New England in the 1630s. Patient notes in his preface that when he went to New England, he was "convinced of the way of *New England*

---

[4] Crawford Gribben, *God's Irishmen* (Oxford: Oxford University Press, 2007), 88.

[5] Underhill adds a question mark next to the date. E. B. Underhill ed., *Confessions of Faith, and other Public Documents, Illustrative of the History of the Baptist Churches of England in the 17th Century* (London: The Hanserd Knollys Society, 1854), 311. Crosby cites that date but does not cite a source to support his claim. See Thomas Crosby, *A History of the English Baptists, from the Reformation to the Beginning of the Reign of King George I* (London: John Robinson, 1740), III, 42.

[6] James Ware, *The Hunting of the Romish Fox and the Quenching of Sectarian Firebrands* (Dublin, 1683), 228.

[7] "At this time many godly Christians going to *New England*, and being come up in my judgment to the way of *New England* in Faith and order, went over thither." Patient, *On the Doctrine*, 6-7.

[8] Thomas Crosby, *A History of the English Baptists* (London: John Robinson, 1740), III, 42.

in Faith and order."⁹ On a side, it is interesting to note that upon his arrival in New England he held to paedobaptism.¹⁰ There is also evidence that a debate arose over the issue of believer's baptism and church membership within the Independent churches in New England. It is possible that he was a minister in New England because, when he returned to England, he quickly rose to the role of an assistant pastor under William Kiffen in London. A quick rise in an influential church seems unlikely for one who had not shown evidence of ministerial experience and calling. However, one could also argue that he was not a minister in New England based on the fact that he directly observed the debate over believer's baptism before he "joined in Communion."¹¹ It is unlikely he would not participate in communion if he were a minister. He also commented that he "attended the preaching of the word"¹² on the subject. He even said that he heard one minister "preach fifteen Sermons on this matter."¹³ Since Patient was listening to preaching but not preaching himself, these comments cast doubt on the claim that Patient was a minister in New England. Rather, it supports the idea that his role with Kiffen was his first vocational ministry experience. Thus, it speaks to Patient's abilities that he would rise so quickly in such an influential church under the leadership of such a significant pastor.

---

⁹ Patient, *On the Doctrine*, 7.

¹⁰ Patient notes that he embraced the "Faith and order" of the Independents in New England and writes, "being not convinced of my error and great darkness in sprinkling the carnal seed of Believers." Patient, *On the Doctrine*, 7.

¹¹ Patient, *On the Doctrine*, 7.

¹² Patient, *On the Doctrine*, 7.

¹³ Patient, *On the Doctrine*, 13.

English Puritan

The Puritans were an outgrowth of the English Reformation. The European Renaissance drove scholars back to classic works and original texts. By returning to the original biblical languages, the Protestant Reformers rediscovered foundational biblical doctrines. They sought to return Christianity back to the authority of the Bible; justification by faith alone rather than good works; salvation by God's grace alone apart from the merits of the sinner; salvation accomplished by Jesus' work on the cross apart from any human merit; and, above all, that this was for the glory of God alone. Martin Luther launched the Protestant Reformation with his *Ninety Five Theses* in 1517. However, the Protestant Reformation gained little traction in England until King Henry VIII sought to annul his marriage. By 1527, Henry sought an annulment from the Pope based on Leviticus 20:21: "If a man takes his brother's wife, it is impurity. He has uncovered his brother's nakedness; they shall be childless." The King's "Great Matter" opened the door for the Protestants in England.

As the years progressed, the Church of England was established and a long series of debates regarding the settlement of the national church continued. Queen Elizabeth I's settlement firmly established a church that attempted to be Protestant in doctrine yet maintain certain Roman Catholic practices. In response, some English Protestants consistently sought to purify the church from these lingering Roman Catholic practices. This movement was religious at its core but had complex political effects. Historically, trying to define the Puritans has been difficult, but most can agree that the Puritans held to a Calvinistic soteriology, an evangelical spirituality, and pursued a biblical ecclesiology.¹⁴ The unique and complex religious settlement in England spawned numerous religious sects. Unity was achieved around certain issues, but differences of interpretations ultimately launched three major Puritan denominations. The Presbyterians, the first, largest, and most significant camp, formed around the idea that the authority of the church lay with a presbytery. There were other Calvinists who believed that the congregation was the ultimate authority of the church. This group was initially labeled "Independents" but ultimately solidified as the Congregationalists. A third Calvinistic group recognized congregational authority but held that only the converted should be members of the congregation. This third group also held to believer's baptism and therefore gained the label "Baptists."

Thomas Patient was an English Puritan of the Calvinistic Baptist sect. This claim is evidenced by the fact that he was one

---

[14] "Firstly, Puritanism was a variety of Protestantism, and Puritans were heirs of the Reformation inaugurated by Martin Luther's seminal re-reading of Christianity's foundational texts. Puritans affirmed the great slogans of Luther's Reformation—*sola fide, sola gratia, sola scriptura*; faith alone, grace alone, scripture alone—though there was disagreement over exactly what these slogans entailed...Secondly, Puritanism was a variety of Reformed Protestantism, aligned with the continental Calvinist churches rather than with the Lutherans...Thirdly, however, Puritanism was a distinctive and particularly intense variety of early modern Reformed Protestantism which originated within the Church of England, and was a product of that unique environment and its tensions." John Coffey and Paul C. H. Lim, eds. *The Cambridge Companion to Puritanism* (Cambridge, England: Cambridge University Press, 2008), 2-3; "The essence of Puritanism... is an experience of conversion which separates the Puritan from the mass of mankind and endows him with the privileges and the duties of the elect." Alan Simpson, *Puritanism in Old and New England* (Chicago: The University of Chicago Press, 1955), 2.

of the fifteen original signers of the *First London Confession*.[15] This Confession was the first of two significant early Calvinistic Baptist confessions of faith. In 1644, Patient was serving in the influential Devonshire Square Church as an assistant pastor to William Kiffen. Patient was at the epicenter of an emerging Baptist movement, which sought to align itself with the larger Calvinistic Puritan sects.

American Baptist

Although Patient was an early English Calvinistic Baptist, his theological journey also passed through the American colonies. Beginning in 1620, Puritans began leaving England to establish colonies in the New World. During the 1630s, around 10,000 people migrated from England to New England. The Pilgrims were primarily Puritans that sympathized with the Separatists and Congregationalists. Beginning with the Plymouth Colony and eventually the Massachusetts Bay Colony, the Pilgrim Fathers established Congregationalism.

In his preface, Patient reports that upon "being convinced of the unwarrantableness of the *Government of the Lordly Prelates, and the Liturgy in the Church of England, and the mixed Communions in the Parish Assemblies*, I was resolved, God willing, to examine all Religion."[16] This examination led him to leave the Church of England and join the Nonconformist

---

[15] William Kiffen, *The Confession of faith of those churches which are commonly (though falsly [sic]) called Anabaptists* (London: Matthew Simmons, 1644), 3.

[16] Patient, *On the Doctrine*, 5.

movement.[17] Patient's evolution resulted in him joining what some have called the "Great Migration" of the 1630s.[18]

Recent discoveries confirm that Patient was in New England in the late 1630s and/or early 1640s. Patient claims to have gone to New England holding to paedobaptism, yet *Records and Files of the Quarterly Court* includes a brief, and rather unique, statement at the Court hearing at Salem on April 27, 1643. The note reads, "Thomas Patience, by a common fame, and upon vehement suspicion, not only of holding, but also of fomenting the error that baptism of infants is no ordinance of God, and hindering his child from baptism. Gone away. Wit: Jno. Ruckman."[19] The New England authorities responded firmly to the acceptance of believer's baptism by Patient and others by establishing a law against baptistic beliefs on November 13, 1644.[20] It is unclear exactly when Patient fled New England, but he was gone by 1643.[21] It is important to note that Patient left England a paedobaptist and returned a Baptist. He was even drawn up on legal charges in New England for his position! This persecution was clearly the reason for his return to

---

[17] Crosby describes Patient as "first an *Independent* minister in *New England*." Crosby, *A History*, III, 42.

[18] "At this time many godly Christians going to *New England*, and being come up in my judgment to the way of *New England* in Faith and order, went over thither." Patient, *On the Doctrine*, 5–6.

[19] Witness of events, John Ruckman. See *Records and Files of the Quarterly Court of Essex County Massachusetts, 1636-1656* (Salem, MA: Essex Institute, 1911), 1:52.

[20] Sidney Lee, ed. *Dictionary of National Biography* (London: Smith, Elder, & Co., 1895), 44:32.

[21] White notes that Patient left "Massachusetts sometime in the late summer of 1642" but does not give documentary support for that date. See B. R. White, *The English Baptists of the Seventeenth Century* (Didcot, England: The Baptist Historical Society, 1996), 72

England. It is also worth noting that the charges were brought against him in 1643, yet only a year later he was serving as an assistant pastor to William Kiffen and signed the *First London Confession*. Patient's American evolution was stark and had a lasting impact on his life. This development in Patient's life will be discussed further in a later section.

English Particular Baptist
Throughout church history, different sects have espoused believer's baptism. One English Puritan Separatist church adopted the practice by 1638. Henry Jacob was the first pastor of the famed Jacob-Lathrop-Jessey (JLJ) church and is best described as a moderate or semi-Separatist. He was critical of the Church of England to the point of writing *Reasons taken out of God's Word and the best human testimonies proving a necessity of reforming our churches in England* in 1604. The book advocates for reforming the Church of England. Jacob's reward for writing it was being thrown into prison. There were at least two other groups that left the JLJ church, likely over Separatists issues and/or believer's baptism, to form other churches.[22] Six people left the church in 1638, desiring a firmer break with the established church so that they could practice believer's baptism.[23] Scholars mark this tiny splinter group as the beginning

---

[22] McBeth quotes the church records: "On September 12, 1633, seventeen persons 'desired dismission that they might become an Entire Church, and further ye communion of those churches in order amongst themselves, which at last was granted to them." Leon McBeth, *The Baptist Heritage: Four Centuries of Baptist Witness* (Nashville: B&H Academic, 1987), 43.

[23] Bebbington states, "Because it nevertheless stood for believer's baptism, it appears to have been the first church that can properly be called Particular Baptist." David W. Bebbington, *Baptists*

of the Calvinistic Baptist movement.[24] This insignificant group was formed around the issue of believer's baptism in 1638, but only six short years later, seven churches signed the monumental *First London Confession*. Likely in 1643, Thomas Patient joined one of these seven churches, as a pastor with William Kiffen at what eventually became the Devonshire Square Church.

The *First London Confession* was intentionally Calvinistic, and thus was an attempt to place these seven churches within the broader Reformed movement. Further, they became known as Particular Baptists as opposed to the General Baptists, signifying that they held to particular redemption. The JLJ church can be categorized as a semi-Separatist congregation, but the groups that splintered off should be defined as Separatist.[25] These groups, particularly the 1638 splinter group, are commonly referenced as the first Particular Baptist congregation.[26] Another doctrinal distinction of these churches

---

Through the Centuries: A History of a Global People (Waco, TX: Baylor University Press, 2010), 46.

[24] McBeth argues, "The most tantalizing statement in the old church minutes says that at their withdrawal in 1633, 'Mr. Eaton with Some others receiving a further Baptism'... In 1638 six more members left this church; they were said to be 'of ye same Judgment with Sam. Eaton about baptism.' Clearly they separated for the sake of baptism of believers... At any rate, historians conclude on the basis of this evidence that definitely by 1638, and possibly by 1633, there was a Particular Baptist church formed in London." McBeth, *The Baptist Heritage*, 44.

[25] McBeth said of Jacob's JLJ church, "Jacob developed a milder form of Separatism, which some have called 'semi-Separatism.'" McBeth, *The Baptist Heritage*, 31.

[26] Lumpkin explains, "The parent church amicably dismissed another group in 1638 whose members held that only regenerated believers should be baptized. This group coming under the leadership

was believer's baptism.[27] They also ultimately affirmed the mode of immersion, noting in Article XL of the *First London Confession*, "The way and manner of the dispensing of this ordinance (c) the Scripture holds out to be dipping or plunging the whole body under water."[28] The emphasis upon baptism had practical implications in that the churches emphasized a regenerate church membership, which held congregational authority particularly in matters of church discipline.[29] Finally, the English Particular Baptists always demonstrated a desire to cooperate for mission endeavors.[30] Patient not only signed the first edition of the *First London Confession*, but he also sought official cooperation with the London Baptist churches when he

---

of John Spilsbery, who meanwhile had become pastor of Eaton's mixed church, is looked upon as the first Particular Baptist Church." William L. Lumpkin, *Baptist Confessions of Faith* (Valley Forge, PA: Judson Press, 1969), 143.

[27] Article XXXIX of the *First London Confession* reads, "That Baptism is an Ordinance of the new Testament, given by Christ, to be dispensed (a) only upon persons professing faith, or that are Disciples, or taught, who upon a profession of faith, ought to be baptized." Lumpkin, *Baptist Confessions*, 167.

[28] Lumpkin, *Baptist Confessions*, 167.

[29] Article XLII of the *First London Confession* reads, "Christ has likewise given power to his whole Church to receive in and cast out, by way of excommunication, any member; and this power is given to every particular Congregation, and not one particular person, either member or Officer, but the whole." Lumpkin, *Baptist Confessions*, 168.

[30] Article XLVII of the *First London Confession* reads, "And although the particular Congregations be distinct and several bodies, everyone a compact and knit city in itself; yet are they all to walk by one and the same rule, and by all means convenient to have the counsel and help one of another in all needful affairs of the Church, as members of one body in the common faith under Christ their only head." Lumpkin, *Baptist Confessions*, 168-169.

established the first Irish Baptist churches.[31] Due to their convictions, the early Particular Baptists sought to govern their own affairs separate from the Church of England.[32]

Family

Although we know nothing of Patient's birth family, it is likely that Patient hailed from the middle class. Patient was heavily involved in the Puritan movement, even going to New England in the 1630s. Others in this movement were part of an emerging middle class rather than the aristocracy. His involvement in the Cromwellian army was primarily because of his Baptist connections, and most of the Baptist ministers had no formal theological training at Oxford or Cambridge. However, Thomas and his wife Sarah did have the financial means to travel to

---

[31] Kreitzer provides the full text of a letter from the Irish Baptists to the London Baptists dates June 1, 1653. In the letter the authors (including Thomas Patient) write, "And to keep a more revived correspondency with each other by letters and loving Epistles." Larry J. Kreitzer, *William Kiffen and his World (Part 2)* (Oxford: Centre for Baptist History and Heritage, Regent's Park College, 2012), 221; White also states, "On 1 June 1653 a letter signed by Thomas Patient and other leaders of the Irish Baptist churches was sent to London with John Vernon... they suggested that the Londoners should send out two or more representatives to visit and instruct local congregations up and down the land." B. R. White, "Thomas Patient in England and Ireland," *Irish Baptist Historical Society Journal*, 2 (1969/70): 41.

[32] Article XXXVI of the *First London Confession* reads, "That being thus joined, every Church has power given them from Christ for their better well-being, to choose to themselves meet persons into the office of Pastors, Teachers (a), Elders, Deacons, being qualified according to the Word, as those which Christ has appointed in his Testament, for the feeding, governing, serving, and building up of his Church, and that none other have power to impose them, either these or any other." Lumpkin, *Baptist Confessions*, 166.

New England and they were able to return upon his acceptance of believer's baptism. These themes suggest Patient was likely part of the emerging middle class and not from any prominent family.

There are only three sources that assist in piecing together Thomas and Sarah's family. First, their wills.[33] Thomas died before Sarah in 1666 and left his entire earthly belongings to her without mention of any children. Likewise, Sarah's will does not mention any children. Instead, she leaves some of her belongings to some women she knows and the rest of her belongings and estate in Ireland to be dispersed to widows by Kiffen and two other men.[34] Second, there is no mention of any of his own children in *On the Doctrine of Baptism*. If Patient was born in the early 1590s and was then in New England in the 1630s, he would have been in his 40s. He and Sarah would have likely had children at that age, and it would be odd for Patient not to mention the state of his own children when giving his biographical account regarding infant baptism. Even though there is no mention of children in his will or his autobiographical account in the preface of *On the Doctrine of Baptism*, there is a mention of a child in *Records and Files of the Quarterly Court*. This document states that charges were brought against Patient for holding "the error that baptism of infants is no ordinance of

---

[33] The wills are included in Kreitzer, *William Kiffen and his World (Part 2)*, 254–257. There is no mention of children in the wills. Thomas simply leaves his entire estate to Sarah: "if my wife be the last liver and do survive me I do make her my whole Executor and give all to her be it little or much." Kreitzer, *William Kiffen and his World (Part 2)*, 254). Likewise, Sarah mentions no children in her will.

[34] Kreitzer, *William Kiffen and his World (Part 2)*, 256.

God."³⁵ The record also states that Patient was "hindering his child from baptism."³⁶ Put together, these sources lead us to conclude that the Patients had at least one child, but the child and any subsequent children preceded them in death.

London

William Kiffen's influence on the start of the Particular Baptist movement cannot be overstated. He was the most influential figure in the movement from its founding in the late 1630s until his death in 1701. The controversial *Kiffin Manuscript* can be interpreted as claiming that Kiffen was part of the group that split from the JLJ church in 1633, desiring a Separatist congregation versus a semi-Separatist church. It is also possible that Kiffen was part of Spilsbury's congregation that began in 1638 over the issue of believer's baptism.³⁷ The final step of evolution took place in 1640 when baptism by immersion was espoused.³⁸ The evidence seems clear that Kiffen was an emerging leader in a movement that evolved into Separatism, believer's baptism, and baptism by immersion. By 1644, seven churches were established and Kiffen was a key leader of the

---

³⁵ *Records and Files of the Quarter Court*, 52.

³⁶ *Records and Files of the Quarter Court*, 52.

³⁷ Torbet explains, "In 1638 others were added, including William Kiffen." Robert Torbet, *A History of the Baptists*, 3rd ed. (Valley Forge: Judson Press, 1963), 42.

³⁸ Torbet also states, "According to Burrage's corrected reading of the Kiffen Manuscript, during 1640 Richard Blunt and certain other members of Spilsbury's and perhaps a few of Jessey's church, became convinced that baptism by sprinkling or pouring, whether administered to believers or adults, or to infants, was not the form baptism 'ought to be by dipping the body into the water, resembling burial and rising again.'" Torbet, *A History*, 42.

movement as well as the pastor of what became the Devonshire Square Church.

The church began sometime after the start of Spilsbury's congregation in 1638 and before the *First London Confession of Faith* in 1644, most likely beginning in 1640. It is probable that the church did not actually begin meeting in Devonshire Square until 1653. Many consider the formation of Spilsbury's congregation in 1638 the first Particular Baptist Church, but Kiffen's congregation was one of the first seven churches.

Their pastor truly was a remarkable man.[39] Even his opponents recognized his influence.[40] In addition to his role at the church, he was an extremely successful businessman, despite having grown up in poverty.[41] Kiffen began in the glove business but became wealthy in the woolen-cloth trade business.

---

[39] Haykin quotes Ivimey: "When Joseph Ivimey (1773-1834), the nineteenth-century Baptist historian, published the life of William Kiffin in 1833 he did so in the conviction that Kiffen was one of the most extraordinary persons whom the [Calvinistic Baptist] denomination has produced, both as to the consistency and correctness of his principles and the eminence of his worldly and religious character." Michael A.G. Haykin, *Kiffen, Knollys and Keach: Rediscovering Our English Baptist Heritage* (Peterborough, Canada: H&E Publishing, 2019), 47. The information was taken from Joseph Ivimey, *The Life of Mr. William Kiffin* (London, 1833), xi, xii.

[40] Nettles quotes from Ivimey who quotes Josiah Ricraft commenting on Kiffen's, *A Looking Glass*. Ricraft describes Kiffen as "the author, and grand ringleader of that seduced sect." Tom Nettles, *The Baptists: Key People Involved in Forming a Baptist Identity: Volume One, Beginnings in Britain* (Ross-shire, Scotland: Christian Focus, 2005), 132.

[41] White says, "He had been orphaned during the plague of 1625 and had been a near penniless apprentice during the years thereafter." White, *English Baptists of the Seventeenth Century* (Didcot, England: The Baptist Historical Society, 1996), 70.

EARLY LIFE & MINISTRY

His wealth opened many high-society doors for him as well as giving a level of credibility for the Particular Baptists. Given such a social position, Kiffen also became influential in the political arena. White notes that Kiffen "became Member of Parliament for Middlesex 1656–1658, Master of the Leathersellers Company of London 1671–1672, and an Alderman of the City in 1687."[42] A common story is told that King Charles II himself came to Kiffen for a loan of 40,000 pounds! The story goes that Kiffen responded not with a loan of 40,000 pounds but a gift of 10,000 pounds. Nettles reports that "Kiffen remarked privately to a friend that he had saved himself 30,000 pounds by such a gift."[43] Kiffen travelled throughout England evangelizing as well as debating Baptist doctrine. McBeth notes, "Perhaps the most famous Baptist disputation was the one held on October 17, 1642, at Southwark. William Kiffen and three other Baptists disputed against Daniel Featley, a leading minister of the Church of England."[44]

Kiffen also engaged in other debates at Coventry. Patient and Kiffen also participated in an evangelistic tour to Kent.[45] He was also a prolific writer, publishing numerous works. Some of his more famous texts include *A Brief Remonstrance*, *A Sober Discourse of Right to Church-Communion*, and *The Life and Death of that Old Disciple of Jesus Christ, the Eminent Minister of the Gospel, Mr. Hanserd Knollys*.

William Kiffen's influence over the entire movement cannot be overstated. He was influential in the Particular Baptists' vision of developing associations around the country with the

---

[42] White, *The English Baptists*, 70.
[43] Nettles, *The Baptists*, 133.
[44] McBeth, *The Baptist Heritage*, 65.
[45] B. R. White, "Thomas Patient," 38.

purpose of evangelism and the start of new churches.[46] Kiffen's influence was also on display as he diffused tensions over the so-called Fifth Monarchy movement. Bell describes the movement as:

> The Fifth Monarchists were the last manifestation of the most forceful millenarian radicalism unleashed by the Reformation. The movement took its name from members' belief that the fifth monarchy, the rule of Christ, and his saints, was at hand. The seventh chapter of Daniel served as their primary proof text.[47]

Many Baptists were sympathetic with the movement's claims. When Oliver Cromwell accepted the title of Lord Protectorate many in the movement were outraged, including some Baptists, thus causing tension between the Baptists and the Cromwellian government. In response to the tension, Kiffen wrote a letter to the Irish Baptists on January 20, 1654, pleading with them to be "subject to all Civil powers they being of god."[48] The letter succeeded and the tensions subsided. Kiffen's influence was once again apparent. Of the seven original churches, Devonshire Square was esteemed due to the

---

[46] This article explains in depth the strategy of the Particular Baptists during the early years of the movement. See B. R. White, "The Organization of the Particular Baptists 1644-1666," *Journal of Ecclesiastical History*, 17 (1966): 209-226.

[47] Mark R. Bell, *Apocalypse How?: Baptist Movements during the English Reformation* (Macon, GA: Mercer University Press, 2000), 164.

[48] Larry J. Kreitzer, *William Kiffen and his World (Part 1)* (Oxford: Centre for Baptist History and Heritage, Regent's Park College, 2010), 39.

stature and notoriety of Kiffen. Patient must have been a gifted man to become Kiffen's assistant so quickly after returning from New England.

First London Confession

The significance of the *First London Confession* is summarized by White when he writes, "Calvinistic Baptists first appeared as a self-conscious group with the publication of their Confession in London in 1644."[49] The Confession established the churches as a group, denomination, and movement. It established theological convictions that continue to distinguish the worldwide contemporary Baptist movement. Patient had an influential ministry serving as Kiffen's assistant pastor, but the *First London Confession* is the most significant portion of his ministry in London.

The Baptist Confession is a partial modification of the Separatist Confession of 1596 (*A True Confession*). The first twenty articles of the 1644 Statement closely mirror the first seventeen articles of the 1596 Statement. The Baptist Confession expands upon the Separatist Statement when addressing the *triplex munus Christi*. The Baptists also add articles twenty-one to thirty-two on the nature of faith and the gospel.[50] These articles are not found in the Separatists' version. Both Confessions address the nature of the church as God's "spiritual Kingdom,"[51] but White rightly concludes that the Baptist Statement "laid less stress upon the distinctive functions of the

---

[49] White, *The English Baptists*, 59.

[50] White describes this section as "dealing with the life of the believer as one of God's elect." White, *The English Baptists*, 64.

[51] The *First London Confession* includes the statement in article XXXIII (Lumpkin, *Baptist Confessions*, 165) and the 1596 includes the statement in article XIIV (Lumpkin, *Baptist Confessions*, 87).

ministry considered apart from the congregation."[52] Article forty-seven from the *First London Confession* mirrors word for word Article 38 of *A True Confession*. The Statement advocates for the ultimate authority of the local congregation, but also advocates for working together. This Statement laid the theological groundwork for future Baptist associations.

In comparison to the Separatists' Statement, the Baptist Confession includes additional articles and doctrines. Firstly, they define the doctrine of believer's baptism by immersion. They uphold believer's baptism by saying that baptism is "only upon persons professing faith."[53] They also say that the mode or manner of baptism is by "dipping or plunging the whole body under water."[54] Secondly, the Baptists explain how they believe the church should relate to the civil Magistrates. In their explanation, they affirm that "Supreme Magistrate of this Kingdom we believe to be the King and Parliament."[55] No doubt the Baptists were very concerned about being associated with the infamous Anabaptist rebellion in Munster.[56] The *First*

---

[52] White, *The English Baptists*, 63.
[53] Lumpkin, *Baptist Confessions*, 167.
[54] Lumpkin, *Baptist Confessions*, 167.
[55] Lumpkin, *Baptist Confessions*, 169.
[56] "The false claims made by Thomas Munzer (1490–1525), a socialist and leader in the Peasants' War of 1525, and the horrors of the Munster Rebellion ten years later under the leadership of Melchior Hofmann and Jan Matthys, combined to bring the Anabaptists into complete disrepute. The extravagant cruelty and wanton destruction of the visionaries who sought to establish the millennial kingdom in the Catholic city of Munster made an indelible impression upon Europeans. The successful suppression of the Rebellion was the signal for nearly all of Europe to intensify the persecution of Anabaptists on the grounds that they, like the fanatics of Munster, were a potential menace to law and order." Torbet, *A History*, 23; "By 1644, however, the rapid growth of Baptist views called forth

London Confession utilizes *A True Confession* as a template for their Statement but adds to it. In summary, the Baptist Statement seeks to establish the movement as Calvinistic, congregational, Baptistic, and as desiring a submissive relationship with civil authorities. Regarding Calvinism, they say they have been wrongly charged with "holding free-will, falling away from grace, denying original sin."[57] Article V reads:

> All mankind being thus fallen, and become altogether dead in sins and trespasses, and subject to the eternal wrath of the great God by transgression; yet the elect, which God hath loved with an everlasting love, are redeemed, quickened, and saved, not by themselves, neither by their own works, lest any man should boast himself, but wholly and only by God of his free grace and mercy through Jesus Christ, who of God is made unto us wisdom, righteousness, sanctification and redemption, that as it is written, He that rejoiceth, let him rejoice in the Lord.[58]

Article XXII also describes faith as "the gift of God wrought in the hearts of the elect by the Spirit of God."[59] Regarding their Congregationalism Article XLII reads:

---

serious opposition to the Baptists and their program. The most serious accusations leveled against them by their enemies were of Pelagianism and anarchy, both of which were associated in the popular mind with the radical wing of the Anabaptist movement of the Continent." Lumpkin, *Baptist Confessions*, 144.
[57] Lumpkin, *Baptist Confessions*, 155.
[58] Lumpkin, *Baptist Confessions*, 158.
[59] Lumpkin, *Baptist Confessions*, 162.

> Christ has likewise given power to his whole Church to receive in and cast out, by way of excommunication, any member; and this power is given to every particular congregation, and not one particular person, either member or officer, but the whole.[60]

This clearly establishes them as Congregationalists, but they also advocate that the particular local congregation has the authority of Christ to "choose to themselves"[61] their pastors and other officers. Differing from the Independent Congregationalists, the Presbyterians, and of course the Anglicans, these English Baptists establish believer's baptism by immersion in Articles XXXIX and XL.

The seven churches were incredibly sensitive to being labeled Anabaptists.[62] The churches were appropriately sensitive because all of England was constantly concerned about anarchy and rebellion. The entire European continent remembered the Anabaptist Munster rebellion of 1534 to 1535 and feared a repeat of history. The Baptists sought to distance themselves from the radical Anabaptists, and in so doing, laid the groundwork for our modern understanding of the separation of Church and State. Articles XLVIII to LII address their desired relationship with their government. Firstly, they recognize that the civil government is an "ordinance of God set up by God for the punishment of evil doers, and for the praise

---

[60] Lumpkin, *Baptist Confessions*, 168.

[61] Lumpkin, *Baptist Confessions*, 166.

[62] Even the title of the Confession expresses this sensitivity. They say this document is the confession of faith of "those Churches which are commonly (though falsly [sic]) called Anabaptists." Lumpkin, *Baptist Confessions*, 156.

of them that do well."⁶³ Secondly, in Article XLVIII they confess their desire and obligation to pray for their civil government as well as to "live a peaceable and quiet"⁶⁴ life "in all godliness and honesty"⁶⁵ under the government's authority. Thirdly, they specifically recognize the authority of King and Parliament in Article XLIX. Fourthly, in Article L they humbly ask for protection as religious minorities. Fifthly, they also confess God's authority over the civil Magistrates and thus confess they will strive to remain faithful to God if the state conflicts with God's teachings. Sixthly, they commit to pay their taxes. Seventhly, in summary, they confess their "desire to give unto God that which is God's, and unto *Cesar* that which is *Cesar's*."⁶⁶

Finally, one of the unique features of the *First London Confession* is the foundation it lays for associational partnership. The Confession's Article XLVII explains their position on associational partnership and is verbatim to Article 38 of *A True Confession*. Article XLVII reads:

> And although the particular Congregations be distinct and several bodies, everyone a compact and knit city in itself; yet are they all to walk by one and the same rule, and by all means convenient to have the counsel and help one another in all needful affairs of the Church, as members of one body in the common faith under Christ their only head.⁶⁷

---

[63] Lumpkin, *Baptist Confessions*, 169.
[64] Lumpkin, *Baptist Confessions*, 169.
[65] Lumpkin, *Baptist Confessions*, 169.
[66] Lumpkin, *Baptist Confessions*, 170–171.
[67] Lumpkin, *Baptist Confessions*, 168–169.

This statement recognizes the authority of the local church body, but also commends individual churches to seek counsel and help from one another. The Independents did not capitalize on this associational idea to the degree that the Baptists did. Partnering for counsel and support became an early mark of the Particular Baptists that survives even into the modern Baptist movement.

Thomas Patient was not just an author and signer of this significant Confession, but he also reflected these convictions in his own personal ministry. His involvement in the movement clearly distinguished him as a Calvinist. The seven churches desired to remain under the broader Reformed umbrella. Regarding Congregationalism, when Patient was in Ireland, he set up self-governing churches based on the authority given to those churches in passages like Matthew 18. *On Baptism* distinguished Patient as espousing believer's baptism by immersion. As shown above, commitment to this doctrine led to great persecution in the American colonies. As will be shown, it also caused him great persecution in Cromwellian Ireland. Patient's relationship to the state will be explored later, but he demonstrated a submission to both God and the State as an Army chaplain. He was actually employed by the State but took advantage of the situation to not only minister to soldiers but also evangelize the Irish and establish the first Irish Baptist churches. We will see that he did not forfeit his prophetic voice even as an employee of the State, but he also showed respectful restraint. Finally, Patient was committed to associational partnerships. When he founded the Irish Baptist churches, he intentionally engaged the influential London Baptist churches. This engagement included a desire for prayer partnerships but also discussion on other significant issues. For example, upon Kiffen's plea, Patient and the other Baptists tempered their outrage over Cromwell accepting the Lord Protector title.

Kent Evangelistic Tour

Patient's involvement in the *First London Confession* is arguably the most significant achievement during his London ministry, but his evangelistic tour to Kent with William Kiffen is worth noting. Kent is a county southeast of London, between the capital and the English Channel. In 1672, Luke Howard published a short account of the origins of the Baptist movement in Kent, entitled *A Looking Glass for Baptists*. Howard was one of the first converts to the Particular Baptist faith. He wrote that Kiffen, along with Patient, "began to have an entrance into Kent"[68] in 1643 and 1644. Anne Stevens (who later became Howard's wife) was the first to be baptized. Later Kiffen baptized Nicolas Woodman, Mark Elfreth, and Luke Howard. It was during this time that Clarkson reports that he went up to London to discuss the issue of believer's baptism and "after a little discourse with Patience, I was by him baptized in the water that runneth about the Tower."[69] But, after these conversions, the General Baptists came into Kent and convinced many of the converts to their doctrine. The issue became contentious, as evidenced by the fact that the General Baptists led some of the converts to be rebaptized, believing that they were previously "baptized into a wrong Faith and another Gospel."[70] These accounts from 1643 to 1644 highlight the nature

---

[68] Luke Howard, *A Looking Glass for Baptists: Being a Short Narrative of their Root and Rice in Kent* (London, 1672), 5.
[69] Laurence Claxton, *The Lost Sheep Found* (London, 1660), 12.
[70] Claxton, *The Lost Sheep*, 5.

of Patient's evangelistic ministry while in London. Many were converted but many were lost to other competing sects. Patient continued his evangelistic and church-starting strategy in Ireland, but the theological battles of the day also followed him there.

2
IRISH MINISTRY

Thomas Patient lived and ministered during the tumultuous years of the English Civil War, which affected all of the British kingdoms. His Irish ministry is the most significant period of his ministry and will be explored at length. Below is a concise overview of the English Civil War as well as Cromwellian Ireland.

The English Civil War

The English Civil War was a series of bloody conflicts between those loyal to the Parliament and those loyal to the King. It was a complex clash of ideas and climax of conflicts rooted in both Reformation-related convictions and Enlightenment-related ideals. The Reformation called for a biblical Protestant faith and thus would not co-exist with any form of popery. As Henry VIII's, Edward VI's, and Elizabeth I's Protestant settlement solidified in the hearts of the English, any hint of popery from the monarch aroused great suspicion from the people. The Enlightenment called for a reexamination of the role of government as for the benefit of the people rather than for the benefit of the monarch. Especially in light of Charles I's incompetence and abuses of power, the English began to desire a monarch that was answerable to a representative Parliament.

The first of three successive wars broke out in 1642 while Patient was most likely still in New England. This portion of the war continued until May 1646 when the King surrendered as a result of the New Model Army's victories. The remaining factions could not work together, and none of the factions were strong enough to dominate the other factions, therefore, an outbreak of war began again in 1648. This second stage of the war concluded with the beheading of Charles I on January 30, 1649. At this stage of the conflict, Patient was serving alongside Kiffen in London.

After Charles I's death, his son was able to garner support from the Scottish Parliament and thus lead their army against Cromwell's forces. In 1649, as Charles II was solidifying power in Scotland, Cromwell was stamping out rebellion in Ireland. Cromwell landed in Ireland in August of 1649 and left in May of 1650 in order to invade Scotland. It was during this season that Thomas Patient travelled to Ireland. Cromwellian forces continued to battle smaller, yet persistent, Irish forces until 1652. Cromwell effectively ended the English Civil War with his victory over Charles II's forces at the Battle of Worcester on September 3, 1651. The Interregnum began when Charles II fled to France and it continued until his return in 1660.

John Owen's Pleadings to Parliament
Understanding how Thomas Patient ended up in Ireland requires an explanation of John Owen's rapid rise to influence. Owen is rightly described as the "prince of Puritans" for his tireless and profound writings.[1] His rise coincides with the rise

---

[1] Andrew Thomson felt the best way to summarize the significance of Owen was through the subtitle of his book. He described Owen as the "Prince of Puritans." Andrew Thomson, "Life of

of Oliver Cromwell, who rose to influence in a power vacuum and ended up the head of the army that supported the Parliamentary cause against King Charles I's, then King Charles II's, forces. Cromwell clearly had Puritan sympathies and viewed his cause as just. He desired for his men not only to win battles but practice godly living. Cromwell brought on Owen as his chaplain, even bringing him to Ireland in 1649.[2] Owen described the spiritual state of Ireland as a "numerous multitude of as thirsting a people after the gospel as ever yet I conversed withal."[3] When Owen returned to England, he preached to Parliament on February 28, 1650 a sermon entitled "Steadfastness of Promises, and the Sinfulness of Staggering." In this sermon, he said, "there was, for the present, one gospel preacher for every walled town in the English possession in Ireland. The

---

Owen," in the *Works of John Owen* (Carlisle, PA: Banner of Truth Trust, 1965), 1:XLII.

[2] Thomson writes: "On the 19th of April we find Owen once more summoned to preach before Parliament, the chiefs of the army being also present; on which occasion he preached his celebrated sermon, 'On the Shaking of Heaven and Earth,' Heb. xii. 27. Oliver Cromwell was present, and probably for the first time heard Owen preach...Owen's tall and stately figure soon caught the eye of Cromwell as the person whom he had heard preach with so much delight yesterday; and going up to him, he laid his hands upon his shoulders, and said to him familiarly, 'Sir, you are the person I must be acquainted with.' Owen modestly replied, 'That will be much more to my advantage than yours.' To which Cromwell returned, 'We shall soon see that;' and taking Owen by the hand, led him into the garden, and made known to him his intention to depart for Ireland, and his wish that Owen should accompany him as chaplain, and also to aid him in investigating and setting in order the affairs of the University of Dublin." Thomson, "Life of Owen," 1:XLII.,

[3] John Owen, *Of the Death of Christ* (1647; Reprint, Carlisle, PA: Banner of Truth Trust, 2000). *The Works of John Owen*, 10:479.

land mourneth and the people perish for want of knowledge."[4] Parliament responded to Owen's pleadings for gospel reform in Ireland by both investing money and land into Trinity College as well as establishing a college in Dublin. In addition, on March 8, 1649, Parliament resolved to "send over six able Ministers, to dispense the Gospel in the City of Dublin: And that two hundred Pounds per Annum be allowed to every Minister respectively."[5] Thomas Patient was one of the six able ministers.

History of Military Campaign & Pre-Fleetwood Years

Oliver Cromwell and his New Model Army landed in Ireland in August of 1649 and began a brutal campaign against Irish Catholics and English Royalists. Virtually no one supported the Parliamentary and Puritan cause in Ireland. Most of the Irish were Catholic and Cromwell needed to defeat them quickly, otherwise they would gain support from other Catholics in the region. The Protestants in Ireland were largely supportive of the King, so Cromwell needed to either defeat them or gain their support. Barnard explains that until the arrival of Henry Cromwell (Oliver's son) in 1655, policy was punitive rather than persuasive, describing that the policies were "aimed less at converting the Irish than at bludgeoning them into submission and leaving them too weak to rise again."[6] Historians still debate the severity of Cromwell's campaign. For example, during the siege of Drogheda most of the 3,000 garrisoned

---

[4] Thomas Russell, ed., *The Works of John Owen* (London: Richard Baynes, 1826), 1:91.

[5] *House of Commons Journal*, 6 (8 March 1649): 379.

[6] T. C. Barnard, *Cromwellian Ireland: English Government and Reform in Ireland 1649–1660* (Oxford: Clarendon Press, 1975), 12.

Royalist soldiers were killed along with many civilians and even Catholic priests. Later in Wexford, over 2,000 soldiers were killed along with over 1,500 civilians and much of the town was destroyed. However, historians debate if Cromwell's actions were consistent with the contemporary siege tactics of the time. Furthermore, Cromwell's forces confiscated Irish lands, resulting in the destruction of the Irish Catholic land-owning class, which led to generations of abuse and the rise of Irish nationalism. In short, after taking Dublin, Cromwell was victorious in Drogheda, Wexford, and Waterford. Cromwell's victories continued until the alliance between the Irish Catholics and the Protestant Royalists fell apart in May of 1650. Cromwell left Ireland in May 1650, leaving command in the hands of Henry Ireton who died the next year. Most of the Irish Catholics' land was confiscated during the reign of Oliver Cromwell and given to those loyal to his cause, including his soldiers. Thomas Patient himself received land during his time in Ireland and this land was later accounted for in his will.

History of Charles Fleetwood Years
Upon Henry Ireton's death, Charles Fleetwood (a religious Independent)[7] became Lord Deputy of Ireland. Interestingly, he also married Ireton's widow, Bridget, who was the daughter of Oliver Cromwell. Baptists had been welcomed into the leadership of Cromwell's army during the campaigns in Ireland and they remained in favor during Ireton's administration. [8]

---

[7] This is evidenced by the fact that his personal chaplain was an Independent named Nathanael Partridge. See Barnard, *Cromwellian Ireland*, 100.

[8] "Baptists first arrived in Ireland in the early 1650's and were composed as a conglomeration of persons attached to the military

Fleetwood was also very sympathetic to the Baptists. He selected them for leadership roles in key areas of civil government, as officers in the army, and even as government-funded chaplains.[9]

By the time Fleetwood was installed in November of 1651, there were two Independent congregations in Dublin.[10] Even though Fleetwood was not a Baptist, he was sympathetic to the idea of religious tolerance. His understanding opened the door for Baptists to flourish. Many of Fleetwood's principal officers strongly supported and even attended congregations with Baptist pastors or with Baptist leanings. Most were always suspicious of the Baptists, but when the Baptist movement began to be perceived as a front for the Fifth Monarchy movement,[11]

---

establishment." Kevin Herlihy, *The Irish Dissenting Tradition, 1650–1750* (Dublin: Four Courts Press, 1995), 68.

[9] Brown writes, "It was natural that under Cromwell and Ireton the Independents and Baptists should have been put into places of trust, and under Fleetwood this tendency continued, in an intensified form, until, with the exception of a few extreme Independents like Fleetwood, Ludlow, Jones, and Hewson, practically the whole administration came to be in the hands of Baptists. A well-informed Independent complained in the fall of 1655 that he knew of at least twelve governors of towns and cities, ten colonels, three or four lieutenant-colonels, ten majors, nineteen or twenty captains, two salaried preachers, and twenty-three officers on the civil list, who were Baptists." Louise Fargo Brown, *The Political Activities of the Baptists and Fifth Monarchy Men in England During the Interregnum* (Oxford: Oxford University Press, 1912), 136–137.

[10] Barnard states, "One, established by Samuel Winter who had come to Dublin as chaplain to the parliamentary commissioners, met in St. Nicholas's church, and flourished throughout the decade. The other, gathered in Christ Church cathedral, had John Rogers as its pastor." Barnard, *Cromwellian Ireland*, 99.

[11] According to Bell, "The Fifth Monarchists were the last manifestation of the most forceful millenarian radicalism unleashed by the

Cromwell and his allies became alarmed. This perception and Fleetwood's tolerance of the Baptists were leading factors in his demise as ruler over Ireland.

History of Henry Cromwell Years

Baptist influence proved to be a double-edged sword. In a season of complex competing agendas, the consensus was that Fleetwood tipped the scales too much in favor of the Baptists.[12] His inability to maintain a workable balance led to his demise and the installation of Oliver Cromwell's fourth son, Henry. Henry Cromwell proved to be a man with the temperament and capacity to maintain the fragile political balance. Later, when Charles II was made King, Henry skillfully maintained his freedom and much of his wealth. He was effectively in charge of Ireland upon Fleetwood's departure in September of

---

Reformation. The movement took its name from members' belief that the fifth monarch, the rule of Christ and his saints, was at hand. The seventh chapter of Daniel served as their primary proof text. From it they determined that the Assyrian, Persian, Greek and Roman empires were the first four monarchies, which preceded the reign of Christ in the fifth monarch. Now that Rome was undone by the Revolution, the fifth monarchy was dawning and no authority save Christ's was legitimately constituted." Mark R. Bell, *Apocalypse How?*, 164.

[12] Herlihy claims, "Unfortunately for the Baptists many other powerful contemporaries saw them and their allies, rightly or wrongly, as a social and political threat which eventually led to a severe recession of Baptist adherents in Ireland by the late 1650's. In fact, many political rivals believed, or chose to believe, that military opposition to the Cromwellian government in Ireland was an 'anabaptist' one." Herlihy, *The Irish Dissenting Tradition*, 68.

1655. The Baptists had become a political problem and Henry's task was to restore balance.[13]

Ireland's new ruler removed some Baptist leaders from influential positions in the government and army, reduced some of the salaries of Baptist chaplains, and sent some Baptist pastors from prestigious posts to rural areas. He ultimately concluded, "I do not think that God has given them a spirit of government; neither is it safe they have much power in their hands."[14] But, there is also evidence of a civil tone between the Baptist leaders and Henry Cromwell. In 1656, William Allen[15] (and probably Patient) paid a friendly visit to Henry Cromwell to "express satisfaction with his management of affairs."[16] Henry reported that they "give me a little fair words to my face, and commend my management of affairs, and my holding forth a just liberty to all fearing God."[17] This begrudging change of heart could be attributed to the London Baptist leaders' pleas for the Irish Baptists' avoidance of the Fifth Monarchy movement in 1653. Baptists had rarely seen this level of political influence and their very brief period of political prestige

---

[13] Barnard says, "Henry Cromwell's wish to favour all parties founded on the Baptists' intransigence." Barnard, *Cromwellian Ireland*, 106.

[14] Barnard, *Cromwellian Ireland*, 107, taken from Thomas Birch, *A Collection of the State Papers of John Thurloe, esq.* (London, 1742), 3:699.

[15] General William Allen was a prominent military and political figure that was converted to the Baptist movement. He was also brother-in-law to General John Vernon (another prominent military and political figure who became a Baptist).

[16] Brown, *The Political Activities of the Baptists and Fifth Monarchy Men*, 163. Taken from *State Papers of John Thurloe*, 5:453, 731.

[17] Birch, *State Papers of John Thurloe*, 5:729.

Irish Ministry

collapsed under Henry Cromwell. However, their political demise left them a purer religious movement.

Part-Time Army Preacher

The Puritans had a desire to evangelize the Irish and their Baptist sect saw an opening in Cromwell's army. In the late 1640s Patient was closely connected to Kiffen in London. Likely due to this connection, he had the opportunity to sail to Ireland as an Army Chaplain. Thomas Patient arrived in Ireland in 1650. While his primary duties as a chaplain were with the army, Patient also had the opportunity to evangelize to the general population. His ministry included the starting of the first Irish Baptist church. By 1651 there is evidence that Patient was being paid as an army chaplain. Larry Krietzer cites a warrant that paid Patient "Fifty-two pounds and sixteen shillings for one hundred- and thirty-two-days pay being ye three days pay in every week respited from ye 22th of April."[18] Kreitzer also shows a warrant for Patient being paid "Forty-two pounds"[19] on February 11, 1653. Oxford University's Bodleian Library houses a Cromwellian army accounting book used during the Irish campaign.[20] This record shows eleven payments to Patient between £36 and 16s to £11 and 4s from January 1653 to December 1654. Even though Henry Cromwell was limiting the power of the Baptists, Kreitzer lists a payment by the level-headed Cromwell "unto Mr Thomas Patience the sum of forty-two pounds for eighty-four days pay for his

---

[18] Kreitzer, *William Kiffen and his World (Part 2)*, 210–211.
[19] Kreitzer, *William Kiffen and his World (Part 2)*, 211.
[20] I was able to photograph these pages during the Fall of 2012. See MS Rawlinson A 208, pages 379, 390, 410, 420, 421, 427, 434, 439, 441, and 453. Kreitzer also transcribes the records in *William Kiffen and his World (Part 2)*, 212–213.

entertainment as preacher to ye Lord Deputy and general officers of ye Army."[21] This record of payments highlights Patient's role (at least on a part-time basis) as an army chaplain.

Initial Kilkenny Ministry

There is a lack of consensus over when Patient actually arrived in Ireland. In 1683 James Ware wrote that Patient arrived with Charles Fleetwood in 1652.[22] Like Ware, Thomas Crosby writes, "He went with general Fleetwood into Ireland, and settled there."[23] However, the majority of the evidence points to Patient arriving in 1650 as Cromwell was drawing his campaign to a close. Kilkenny was one of the closing victories for Cromwell and Patient was found in Kilkenny around the time that the New Model Army seized control.[24] The most helpful evidence for Patient's presence in 1650 is a letter he sent to Oliver Cromwell on April 15, 1650, immediately after Cromwell left Ireland.[25]

---

[21] Kreitzer, *William Kiffen and his World (Part 2)*, 213.
[22] Kreitzer, *William Kiffen and his World (Part 2)*, 199.
[23] Thomas Crosby, *A History of the English Baptists, from the Reformation to the Beginning of the Reign of King George I* (London: John Robinson, 1740), 3:42–43.
[24] Cromwell concluded the Irish Campaign by securing the southeastern portion of the country. His desire was to secure port cities like Kilkenny, Wexford, and Waterford. Cromwell was excessively cruel as he defeated some cities but lenient on other cities. By 1650 the alliance between English Royalists and Irish Confederates was disintegrating. Kilkenny was the capital for the Irish Confederates. The city surrendered to Cromwell in the Spring of 1650.
[25] Kreitzer, *William Kiffen and his World (Part 2)*, 214–216.

IRISH MINISTRY

This letter, sent on April 15, 1650, is the best evidence of Patient's early presence in Ireland.[26] Patient had great affection for Cromwell, even expressing his "love towards you as one Elect and precious in the sight of god, and one whom god hath honored with higher dignity and honors then ye of this world which is but as the fading flower of the grass."[27] He also notes his "constant prayers"[28] for Cromwell, particularly for the condition of his heart. In his letter, Patient also speaks highly of Cromwell's daughter Bridget. He describes Lady Ireton as one that he could discern "the power of god's grace in her soul."[29] It is interesting to note that even though he would later conflict with Henry Cromwell, he speaks very highly of him in this letter to Oliver. Finally, Patient makes an intimate note about the improving health of Oliver's grandchild.

Patient's letter to Oliver Cromwell was dated April 15, 1650, and we also have a warrant for payment to Patient for his work as a chaplain beginning April 22, 1650.[30] Kreitzer notes that this warrant pays him as an army chaplain for three days per week, thus freeing him to establish a Baptist church the other days.[31] These sources show that Thomas Patient was in Kilkenny during the Spring of 1650 working part-time as an

---

[26] "My Lord from ye little acquaintance I had with your excellency before you went out of Ireland, and ye suitableness that I found in that little of your experiences which I was made partakers of Compared with my observation of the goings of God with you for many years." Kreitzer, *William Kiffen and his World (Part 2)*, 214.

[27] Kreitzer, *William Kiffen and his World (Part 2)*, 214.

[28] Kreitzer, *William Kiffen and his World (Part 2)*, 215.

[29] Kreitzer, *William Kiffen and his World (Part 2)*, 215.

[30] Kreitzer, *William Kiffen and his World (Part 2)*, 210-211.

[31] Kreitzer, *William Kiffen and his World (Part 2)*, 200.

army chaplain and establishing the first Irish Baptist churches with his remaining time.

First Irish Baptist Church (Waterford/Kilkenny)
During the Spring of 1650, Thomas Patient set about ministering to army leaders as well as evangelizing the Irish population. Waterford is a town on the southern coast of Ireland. It sits directly across the Suir River from Kilkenny. We know, based on his letter to Oliver Cromwell, that Patient was in this region of the country in the Spring of 1650. Apparently, his work was effective because, by January of 1651, he was pastoring an established church of believers in Waterford.

This church, pastored by Patient, clearly espoused believer's baptism. Therefore, this congregation is considered the first Baptist church in Ireland. The best evidence we have for the existence of this church and its identity is a letter the church sent to Christ Church in Dublin on January 14, 1651. A reprinting of the letter can be found in John Roger's book *Ohel*[32] published in 1653. Patient, along with eleven other men, signed and sent the letter. Firstly, the fact that twelve men were organized enough to send a letter in January of 1651 means that it can be assumed that the church was actually constituted in 1650. Secondly, the content of the letter was addressing the issue of believer's baptism by immersion. Therefore, it can be reasonably understood that this church in Waterford felt believer's baptism by immersion was a central tenet of their church. Why else would they rebuke another church on their stance on believer's baptism by immersion if they did not

---

[32] John Rogers, *Ohel: A Tabernacle for the Sun: or Irenicum Evangelicum, An Idea of Church-Discipline* (London, 1653), 302–306. This letter is also available in the appendix below, pages 129–132.

feel passionately about the doctrine? They address the church in Dublin as "Beloved Friends"[33] and recognize that they "professedly *put on* the Lord Jesus Christ by Baptism."[34] Patient's Waterford church rebuked this group within the Dublin church because they were "joined in fellowship with such as do fundamentally differ in judgement and practice; to wit, such as agree not with you about the true state of a visible Church, nor the fundamental Ordinances thereof."[35] The letter even goes so far as to advocate division from fellowship on the ground of not adhering to believer's baptism by immersion. They write:

> but the very end of Church-fellowship is the observation of all Christ's command, as the Commission holds forth; but this your practise, crosseth in that you agree to walk with such as have not, nor practise the Ordinance of dipping Believers, and by your communion with them in Church-administrations, you are made guilty of their sin of disobedience.[36]

To conclude, Patient organized a church in Waterford around Particular Baptist convictions. This church was the first Baptist church in Ireland. This accomplishment was among Patient's most significant. The congregation was also successful in converting two military governors, an impressive feat for a fringe sect.[37] As modern Irish Baptists seek to

---

[33] Rogers, *Ohel*, 302.
[34] Rogers, *Ohel*, 302.
[35] Rogers, *Ohel*, 302.
[36] Rogers, *Ohel*, 304.
[37] Barnard explains, "By April 1650 he was in Kilkenny. His preaching had great effect in Waterford and Kilkenny, where the

understand their identity, they can look to Thomas Patient as the father of their movement. Jesus taught that even though it is men who preach, it is Jesus who builds his church.[38] It is a delight to report that at the writing of this essay, over 360 years after Patient founded this local church, they continue to embrace biblical doctrine, their Baptist identity, and are shining a gospel light into their city.[39]

---

military governors (Lawrence and Axtell respectively) were converted." Barnard, *Cromwellian Ireland*, 101.

[38] Jesus says to Peter in Matthew 16:18, "And I tell you, you are Peter, and on this rock, I will build my church, and the gates of hell shall not prevail against it."

[39] To learn more about the first Baptist church in Ireland visit www.waterfordbaptist.ie/.

3
DUBLIN MINISTRY

Division at Christ Church with John Rogers
Thomas Patient's letter and message were successfully received by a small group of seven or eight within Christ Church in Dublin. John Rogers was leading the congregation. He was an Independent minister who held to infant baptism and open communion. Both doctrines were anathema for Particular Baptists like Thomas Patient. Patient wrote a letter rebuking those who sided with Rogers. His letter was published in the book authored by John Rogers entitled *Ohel*. In his letter, Patient argues from the Great Commission of Matthew 28:19-20 that they were to "observe whatsoever Christ had commanded; that is, as we understand, all the Laws of God's house, the baptised person is to submit unto, and by the Ministers taught the observation of, and this Order is binding."[1] He also rebuked them saying, "you are made guilty of their sin of disobedience, you willingly having communion with them in Church-administrations."[2] Kreitzer explains:

---

[1] John Rogers, *Ohel: A Tabernacle for the Sun: or Irenicum Evangelicum, An Idea of Church-Discipline* (London, 1653), 303.
[2] Rogers, *Ohel*, 304.

The substance of the letter was a stern exhortation to Rogers and his congregation concerning their baptismal theology and their open-membership policy. It called for the members of the church who had been baptized as believers to withdraw fellowship from those who had not.[3]

Patient and his new church in Waterford called for this small group in Dublin to walk no longer with the larger Independent church but rather separate from them.[4] The group heeded the rebuke, and thus Patient's letter caused a church split.[5]

Rogers argued against Patient's reasoning. He claimed the baptism that was referenced in the Great Commission was "executed by Christ's power, i.e. by the Spirit."[6] Rogers understood this baptism as the same "baptism of the Spirit"[7] from 1 Corinthians 12:13. Rogers decried Patient's views as uncharitable and even unchristian.[8] He also claimed that Patient and his group "bruited abroad scurrilous and scandalous reports of many of us."[9] While Christians in past centuries spoke and

---

[3] Larry J. Kreitzer, *William Kiffen and his World (Part 2)* (Oxford: Centre for Baptist History and Heritage, Regent's Park College, 2012), 198.

[4] Patient wrote, "we hear that you do not walk up orderly together, but are joined in fellowship with such as do fundamentally differ in judgement and practice." Rogers, *Ohel*, 302.

[5] Kreitzer explains, "In the end, the letter caused a split within the Dublin church, and prompted seven or eight of the Baptists to withdraw and form their own fellowship which met privately on Sundays." Kreitzer, *William Kiffen and his World (Part 2)*, 198.

[6] Rogers, *Ohel*, 304.

[7] Rogers, *Ohel*, 304.

[8] Rogers, *Ohel*, 305-306.

[9] Rogers, *Ohel*, 307.

wrote with a much harsher tone than is acceptable today, it is clear nonetheless that the feud became very heated.[10] This conflict led to the end of Roger's pastorate of the congregation in Dublin. He left Ireland and arrived back in London by March of 1652.[11] Krietzer reports, "Rogers harbored some resentment against Thomas Patient and other Particular Baptists who supported the closed-communion position, including William Kiffen and his church in London."[12]

White references this debate over baptism and closed communion through a letter by Colonel Jerome Sankey, who questioned the validity of his own baptism.[13] He was baptized as an infant yet questioned its validity because he questioned the faith of his parents. He was a Colonel in Cromwell's Army and crossed paths with Thomas Patient, who ended up baptizing him. White also records the response of Colonel John Jones regarding Patient's views on believer's baptism and closed-communion:

> Let every man do as he is persuaded in his own heart, but let no man despise his brother that hath not attained to his light, or withdraw his communion with him, because he submits not his judgement to him; the communion and fellowship of saints in the ordinances of Christianity is one of the most principle parts of its privileges and enjoyment in the flesh, and the greatest tyranny that can be exercised upon any member of Christianity is to debar him from those privileges and enjoyments upon the act of being

---

[10] White describes Rogers' response as "baffled disgust." White, *The English Baptists*, 39.
[11] Kreitzer, *William Kiffen and his World (Part 2)*, 198.
[12] Kreitzer, *William Kiffen and his World (Part 2)*, 198.
[13] White, *The English Baptists*, 40.

different in judgement or upon any account for which our heavenly father will not keep him out of heaven, and yet in [is?] ye prejudice I have against these men who otherwise are very precious praying people.[14]

History reports numerous accounts of Baptists being persecuted for their baptistic theology, Thomas Patient included. In this case, however, it was Patient himself who caused division in the church over his Particular Baptist convictions. Even Baptists might conclude that Patient was inappropriately divisive over the issue of believer's baptism.

As the Cromwellian program progressed in Ireland, the Baptists gained political power amongst the Army officers. Patient's influence increased from 1650 to 1652. In December 1652, he was called up from Kilkenny and Waterford to Dublin. He was even provided a house with a small lot to grow his own food.[15] He became a preacher at Christ Church Cathedral, the very congregation he rebuked the previous year.[16] The Puritans believed firmly in the preaching ministry. In the coming decades, they would establish salaries for preaching lectureships. Patient was not what we would understand as the Senior Pastor of Christ Church Cathedral, but rather joined a rotation of preachers. This rotation also included Independent preachers. Kreitzer explains that he was also a "member of a group of seven ministers deputed to investigate and offer advice about the best way to promote the preaching of the gospel in Ireland."[17] Despite zealously advocating believer's baptism to the degree of causing division, from 1650 to 1652 Thomas Patient

---

[14] White, *The English Baptists*, 40.
[15] White, *The English Baptists*, 41.
[16] Kreitzer, *William Kiffen and his World (Part 2)*, 198.
[17] Kreitzer, *William Kiffen and his World (Part 2)*, 198.

established the first Baptist church in Ireland, and then rose to the influential position of preacher at Christ Church Cathedral.

Ministry & Building at Swifts Alley, Dublin

Closely following Cromwell's takeover of Dublin, two Independent congregations were established. Dunlop explains, "We know that by October 1651 there were at least two gathered congregations of Independents in Dublin. One was established by Samuel Winter and worshipped in St. Nicholas' Church. The other met in Christ Church cathedral, where John Rogers was a pastor."[18] Out of the congregation that Rogers was leading, Patient took a splinter group and started what would become the first Baptist church in Dublin. The congregation saw quick success. White explains that the congregation "seems to have grown very fast."[19] He also explains that the congregation attracted some prominent figures in Dublin at the time. White states, "even the wife of the Provost of Trinity College, Dr. Samuel Winter, was almost won over."[20] Thomas Patient was the founding pastor of the first Baptist church in Ireland. Adding to his list of accomplishments, the church in Dublin also built the first Baptist structure in Ireland. White explains, "In the following year the first Baptist meeting house in Ireland was erected in Swift's Alley, Dublin under the auspices to house the congregation which had presumably grown from the original splinter from Roger's Independent Church."[21] Swift's Alley was a section of the city of Dublin.

---

[18] Robert Dunlup, "Dublin Baptists from 1650 Onwards," *Irish Baptist Historical Society Journal*, 21 (1988/89): 6.
[19] White, "Thomas Patient," 41.
[20] White, "Thomas Patient," 41.
[21] White, "Thomas Patient," 41.

Even though the congregation saw early growth, not everyone was supportive of the effort. There are reports stating that this Baptist church was harassed. White notes:

> There was certainly a sharp reaction to its initial success and, in 1653, the Council was informed that "several persons of unquiet spirits and lewd conversation have of late used many uncivil demeanours towards Mr. Patient and others who walk with him in the worship of God, railing at and cursing them, and casting stones at them, and some of the said evil persons intended to destroy them by shooting at them."[22]

It was during this season of pastoring the Dublin church that Patient wrote *On Baptism*. Clearly Patient was addressing hostility towards his views on believer's baptism by immersion. His book is a defense of his position as well as an incredibly early text on the topic. Patient pastored the church until October 1655 when "he handed over the responsibility of the Baptist church in Dublin to Christopher Blackwood, and embarked on a missionary journey up and down Ireland."[23] This first church in Dublin still exists and thrives as Grosvenor Road Baptist Church.[24]

Irish Associations & Cooperation with London

Patient's Irish ministry also included intentional efforts to organize all the Irish Baptist churches as well as deliberate efforts to cooperate with the London Baptist churches connected with William Kiffen. For Baptist historians interested in Baptist

---

[22] White, "Thomas Patient," 41.
[23] Krietzer, *William Kiffen and his World (Part 2)*, 198.
[24] Cf. grosvenorbaptist.org.

distinctives, these points are significant. The British Particular Baptist movement was not merely made up of churches that simply shared an ecclesiology. They were a group that had deep relational connections, reaching the degree that they sought counsel from each other and felt the conviction to rebuke each other. They were also churches that sought to partner together to spread the gospel and plant churches. Patient's vision for evangelism included organizing churches within geographic associations as well as partnering with other likeminded Baptist churches.

On June 1, 1653, Patient was in Dublin and was one of the authors of a letter sent to the London Baptist churches. They confessed their regret over their "long silence"[25] to the London churches. The Irish Baptists made four proposals to the London Baptists. White explains:

> First, they suggested a national day of fasting and prayer every month. Secondly, they suggested the resumption of brotherly correspondence. Thirdly, they asked for a list of all the congregations in communion with the London leaders. Finally, they suggested that the Londoners should send out two or more representatives to visit and instruct local congregations up and down the land.[26]

White also explains that all of the proposals were "adopted although only the first seems to have been wholly new."[27] However, these attempts at cooperation were not done in a vacuum separate from larger political forces. Bell explains

---

[25] Krietzer, *William Kiffen and his World (Part 2)*, 219.
[26] White, "Thomas Patient," 41.
[27] White, "Thomas Patient," 41.

that the letter also revealed "the sustained eschatological hopes of the Irish Baptists in the months before the failure of the Barebones Parliament."[28] The timing was significant because after the Barebones Parliament collapsed over disputes between radical and moderate members, Cromwell was named Lord Protector. This title was largely the basis for the rise of the Fifth Monarchy movement.

When Oliver Cromwell accepted the title of Lord Protector, many radicals became very concerned. They were concerned that the title was a step toward a monarchy and they were concerned that the title should be reserved for Christ. Bell writes, "For many, the Protectorate looked uncomfortably similar to the monarchy that God had so recently called them to overthrow. The Saints were extremely dissatisfied."[29] This title led to an erosion of support from Independents and Baptists, even though they had served in the Army under Cromwell. The name "The Fifth Monarchy" comes from the book of Daniel, which teaches that a Fifth Messianic kingdom would come after the Babylonian, Persian, Macedonian, and Roman empires. This faction believed an earthly monarchy would conflict with their allegiance to their heavenly king. Cromwell and his supporters grew concerned as some in this faction flirted with the idea of a violent overthrow of Cromwell. Bell explains that there was an outcry against the Protectorate amongst many Baptists, even London Baptists, but "the Baptists in Ireland shouted the loudest."[30]

---

[28] Mark R. Bell, *Apocalypse How?: Baptist Movements during the English Reformation* (Macon, GA: Mercer University Press, 2000), 151–152.

[29] Bell, *Apocalypse How?*, 153.

[30] Bell, *Apocalypse How?*, 154.

Kiffen was an astute leader, even in the realm of politics, and he feared the Baptists would lose the tolerance of the Protectorate if they became too aligned with the Fifth Monarchists.[31] In response to this emerging alignment, Kiffen sent a letter to his Irish brethren "chastising their protests and demanding their immediate, unqualified acquiescence to the present government."[32] Kiffen went so far as to insist that the churches connected to Patient should not participate in any political activities that would negatively impact the other Baptist churches. He knew that if the Irish churches revolted against the Protectorate, then it would harm the greater movement. In his letter, Kiffen made the case that the "Protectorate was a legitimate government that had saved the country from chaos posed by radical millenarians."[33] Bell explains that Kiffen "urged the Irish Baptists to abandon Fifth Monarchist sympathies, insisting that 'we are clearly satisfied' that if 'the principles held forth by those…of the fifth monarch' had been pursued, they 'would have brought as great a dishonor to the name of God, and shame and contempt to the whole nation, as we think could have been imagined.'"[34] These were certainly strong words for his Baptist brethren. Kiffen concluded his letter by saying:

> This we can say, that we have not had any occasion of sorrow on this matter from any of the churches in

---

[31] Bell writes, "But for Kiffen and his circle, this was simply another government that had to be appeased in order to preserve the de facto toleration that they had gained." Bell, *Apocalypse How?*, 153-154.
[32] Bell, *Apocalypse How?*, 154.
[33] Bell, *Apocalypse How?*, 154.
[34] Bell, *Apocalypse How?*, 154-155.

this nation, with whom we have communion; they with one heart desiring to bless God for their liberty, and with all willingness to be subject to the present authority. And we trust to hear the same from you.[35]

The letter was a clear and thoughtful case for submission to the Protectorate. It was also a correction regarding the path he feared the Irish Baptists were traveling.

Thomas Patient desired for the churches he started to associate together in what would formalize into a denomination. He led groups of churches to relate with each other and partner together in ministry endeavors including starting new churches. Patient also had a track record of leading his congregation to rebuke other congregations. He desired relationship and counsel from the London churches, but he also felt emboldened to admonish them for not engaging the Irish churches. However, Patient also took correction from these leaders and churches with whom he networked. It is unclear if Patient was sympathetic to the Fifth Monarchy movement. What is clear is that he heeded Kiffen's warning and correction. The Irish Baptists received Kiffen's counsel and relations with the Protectorate improved. Kreitzer records a complimentary letter to Oliver Cromwell from the Irish Baptists (including Thomas Patient) dated 1657.[36] Patient's letter concludes:

We shall only further add, that we do assure your Highness, that whatsoever report you have heard of either the Church baptized in Dublin or any other Church in ye same faith in Ireland. It is far from our

---

[35] Bell, *Apocalypse How?*, 155.
[36] Kreitzer, *William Kiffen and his World (Part 2)*, 248–250.

hearts to disown the Lord's Authority in your Highness, or his work in your hand; but that you have with Cordial & endeared Affections been in our hearts, and the weight of your burden and work hath (by the prayers and tears (we can truly say) of the most unsatisfied Brother amongst us) been borne before the Lord & ye throne of his Grace, and we are persuaded shall be so him.[37]

Patient truly embraced genuine partnership in ministry. He was faithful to correct, but also humble to receive correction. He gave advice, but he also took advice.

---

[37] Kreitzer, *William Kiffen and his World (Part 2)*, 249.

4
ON BAPTISM

Thomas Patient's lasting significance is his publication of *On Baptism* in 1654. This was part of his Irish ministry and must be understood in that context. His book is part of his battle for the establishment of Baptist churches in Ireland. The book is one of the first comprehensive treatments of believer's baptism by immersion from the Particular Baptists. *On Baptism* was printed by Henry Hills, a member of Kiffen's church, who published other Particular Baptist books during the Cromwellian era.

Overview of *On Baptism*

On Baptism, larger than a booklet at 179 pages, includes a clear introduction and a listing of the main sections of the book. While there are fifty-eight topics in total, it can be divided into six topical sections. After the introduction, pages 1–28 make up a section devoted to Patient's basic theology of believer's baptism. In pages 29–44 he develops a theology of two distinct covenants. Next, he delves further by addressing the Covenant of Works, including his seven arguments, from pages 44–70. On page 70 he transitions into discussing the Covenant of Grace. Then, from pages 101–168 he provides a lengthy section where he addresses particular passages of Scripture that relate to believer's baptism. He concludes his book with a ten-page section addressing issues related to Baptist ecclesiology.

Introduction & Testimony

Patient opens the work with an introduction that explains his purpose in writing the book and tells his journey to the Baptist faith. He begins with a sense of urgency to his life itself, even citing John 9:4: "for the night cometh when no man can work."[1] His motive for writing was for "God's glory and the service of his generation in this pilgrimage."[2] Patient explains that many books are written and can play on the fleshly carnal hearts of men, but his plan was to simply provide "clear Scripture-evidence"[3] for his argument.

From his opening remarks, Patient moves on to explain his testimony and journey from an unbeliever in England, to a Puritan in America, to a Baptist in England, to becoming a missionary in Ireland. As a Calvinist, he describes his conversion as when "it pleased God to reveal his Son in me, and to work a change in my heart."[4] The date of his conversion is unknown, but he was in England when he became a Christian. After his conversion to Christ, he reports that he was also "converted from the Church of England."[5] Patient identifies his faith with the Pilgrim Fathers who were going to New England. This identification means that he was most likely a Congregationalist. Due to his identification with New England theology, he "went over thither."[6] He explains how, while in New England,

---

[1] Patient, *On the Doctrine*, i.
[2] Patient, *On the Doctrine*, ii.
[3] Patient, *On the Doctrine*, ii.
[4] Patient, *On the Doctrine*, iii.
[5] Patient, *On the Doctrine*, v.
[6] Patient, *On the Doctrine*, vi.

he diligently sought the Scriptures on the issue of believer's baptism. Ultimately, he says:

> Finding my carnal part to desire satisfaction in Infant-baptism: but the more I conferred with, or heard any preach for it, the more was I convinced of the folly and ignorance of the judgment and practice.[7]

This change in his theology resulted in there "being a Warrant at this time issued out to apprehend and bring [him] before the General Court in *New England*."[8] This legal action against Patient resulted in him, similar to Roger Williams, having to flee to the "Woods in that Wilderness"[9] and ultimately escape back to England.

Patient closes his testimony by claiming that the Devil himself was misleading people to believe infant baptism. He also claims that it is Satan behind those who attack Baptists on the grounds that they were somehow related to the violent Anabaptist of Munster, Germany. Patient pleads with the reader not to read his book with a "heart prejudiced"[10] before then signing off as an "Unworthy Servant."[11]

Theology of Believer's Baptism

Patient spends the first five pages of his book examining Pentecost by explaining Acts 2:37-38. Regarding the tongues of fire, he observes that the inner spiritual transformation of those

---

[7] Patient, *On the Doctrine*, xii.
[8] Patient, *On the Doctrine*, xiii.
[9] Patient, *On the Doctrine*, xiii.
[10] Patient, *On the Doctrine*, xvii.
[11] Patient, *On the Doctrine*, xvii.

present was "signified by the outward sign."[12] He walks through the conversion experiences at Pentecost and notes that the preaching of the gospel "is a special means to convert Souls"[13] and that they were converted by a "prick in the heart."[14] Patient follows the logic of the passage and concludes a "true converted soul is an obedient Soul."[15] As such, the converts then ask what they should do now. Peter replies, "Repent, and be baptized."[16] Using this passage, Patient concludes that "it is the duty of every man that believes and repents, to be baptized."[17] Patient's first point about biblical baptism is that genuine believers should be baptized.

Next, from pages 5–17, using Matthew 28:19-20, Patient explains the ministers/ministry, form, name, and subject of baptism. Based on the Great Commission, he describes those ministers who have a baptism ministry as "preaching Disciples."[18] They preach the gospel (described as the "Doctrine of Faith and Repentance"[19]) and thus bring a soul "up to God."[20] He also explains that "justifiable"[21] ministers are the ones that convert souls and disciple to obedience, i.e. baptism. Patient then argues that the form of baptism is to be "dipping, and, as it were, by drowning, overwhelming, or burying in water, and not by sprinkling with water."[22] In typical Baptist fashion, he

---

[12] Patient, *On the Doctrine*, 2.
[13] Patient, *On the Doctrine*, 4.
[14] Patient, *On the Doctrine*, 4.
[15] Patient, *On the Doctrine*, 5.
[16] Patient, *On the Doctrine*, 5.
[17] Patient, *On the Doctrine*, 5.
[18] Patient, *On the Doctrine*, 6.
[19] Patient, *On the Doctrine*, 6.
[20] Patient, *On the Doctrine*, 6.
[21] Patient, *On the Doctrine*, 7.
[22] Patient, *On the Doctrine*, 8.

explains that the term used for "baptism" in Matthew 28 "doth in proper English signify to Dip"[23] and, furthermore, that the Greek, Latin, and English translations all agree on this point. He notes that when the New Testament references baptism, the preposition it uses is "in" or "into" rather than "with."[24] Practically, Patient also references that Philip immersed the Eunuch in Acts 8 and John needed enough water to perform baptism by immersion in John 3. Theologically, referencing Galatians 3 and Romans 6, he also outlines that immersion "appears from the nature of the Ordinance"[25] because the "person that submitteth thereto, doth visibly put on Christ Jesus the Lord, and is hereby visibly planted into his Death, holding forth therein a lively similitude and likeness unto his Death."[26] He concludes that baptism by the form of immersion is a sign that signifies our salvation.[27] Patient additionally illustrates that, according to the Great Commission, baptism is to be done in the name of the three persons of the Trinity (Father, Son, and Spirit) and the subject being baptized must only be a believer. He defines a believer as a "taught and repentant person."[28]

Next, from pages 17–20, Patient outlines another key aspect of his theology of believer's baptism. He writes, "Faith and repentance go before baptism."[29] Patient concludes this because when Matthew 29:19 refers to "them" who are to be discipled and baptized, it is a reference to those that have been

---

[23] Patient, *On the Doctrine*, 8.
[24] Patient, *On the Doctrine*, 8–9.
[25] Patient, *On the Doctrine*, 11.
[26] Patient, *On the Doctrine*, 11.
[27] Patient, *On the Doctrine*, 13.
[28] Patient, *On the Doctrine*, 17.
[29] Patient, *On the Doctrine*, 17.

taught the gospel and have repented of their sins. Using Peter's teaching from Acts 10, he explains that those who should be baptized are those that Christ has "poured down the Spirit upon."[30] Patient summarizes the Apostles' ministries by saying that they "converted men by preaching, and then baptized them."[31]

Patient then steps into what, contemporarily, may be perceived as his more controversial views on believer's baptism. Firstly, he addresses why he disagrees with different aspects of paedobaptism. To do so, Patient first addresses the household baptisms in Acts. Essentially, he argues that "these families were all converted disciples."[32] Regarding the household of Lydia from Acts 16, Patient notes that the household was part of the group described as "brethren" at the end of the chapter (Acts 16:40). Next, he outlines his understanding of the conversion of the Philippian jailer's household in the same chapter. Patient explains from Acts 16:32-34 that the "whole household of the jailor heard the word of God, and rejoiced, and believed as well as the jailor."[33] These examples highlight Patient's belief that no unbelievers, including infants, were baptized in the household accounts in Acts.

Next, Patient addresses what he calls "that idol of sprinkling of carnal poor infants."[34] He explains that an idol is "either the worshipping of a false God, or the true God in a false

---

[30] Patient, *On the Doctrine*, 17.
[31] Patient, *On the Doctrine*, 19.
[32] Patient, *On the Doctrine*, 20.
[33] Patient, *On the Doctrine*, 23.
[34] Patient, *On the Doctrine*, 23.

manner."³⁵ He believed that infant baptism was idolatry of the second kind, even labeling it "man's invention."³⁶

Finally, from pages 24-28, Patient states that the Covenant of Life (eternal life) is made with believers. He defines paedobaptism as the view which sees the Covenant of Grace as belonging to believers and their children and, consequently, that sees baptism as also belonging to those children. This final section on his theology of believer's baptism serves as the transition to the majority of the rest of the book where he addresses the distinctions between the Covenant of Grace and the Covenant of Works.

Two Distinct Covenants

Patient outlines the rest of his work on page 28. He addresses the distinctions between the Covenant of Grace and of Works in pages 29-44, then addresses the Covenant of Works in seven arguments from pages 44-70, before focusing on the Covenant of Grace from pages 70-101. Finally, before his summary, Patient also addresses particular Scriptures from pages 101-168.

Regarding the distinctions between what he describes as the Covenant of Grace and the Covenant of Works, his main point is to explain one as absolute and the other as conditional. Using Jeremiah 31, Patient begins by arguing that there are two distinct covenants. He labels the Covenant of Grace as the Covenant of Life (or eternal life) and describes it as new and "absolute."³⁷ Patient says of Jesus Christ that he is "the peculiar Minister of the New Covenant, (unto the Church then gathered all those that are in Christ, being God's Israel,

---

[35] Patient, *On the Doctrine*, 24.
[36] Patient, *On the Doctrine*, 24.
[37] Patient, *On the Doctrine*, 30.

Abraham's seed)."[38] Patient places all of the Old Testament under the Old Covenant of Works and considers it "conditional"[39] in nature.

Under the New Covenant, Patient explains that faith and repentance are not conditional because they are not obtained "by their own abilities."[40] Rather, he considers both faith and repentance to be gifts from God. Under this New Covenant of Grace, Patient distinguishes it from the Old Covenant of Works by explaining that the New "was never entailed upon any fleshly line or generation, as the Covenant of Circumcision was."[41] At this point, theologically, Patient is distinguishing the New Covenant from circumcision, which he considered part of "a Covenant in the flesh."[42] By citing Paul in Romans 4, Patient argues that the covenant leading to eternal life has nothing to do with circumcision. He describes circumcision as a conditional "covenant of works."[43] He also concludes that circumcision was temporal because it was only considered everlasting "for the Ever of the Law for the time of the Jewish State."[44] In conclusion, Patient believed the Old Testament was part of a distinct Covenant of Works that was conditional and temporal in nature and was not part of the Covenant of Life or Grace because it did not secure eternal life. Circumcision, according to Patient, was a tenet of the old, conditional, temporal, Covenant of Works.

---

[38] Patient, *On the Doctrine*, 30.
[39] Patient, *On the Doctrine*, 30.
[40] Patient, *On the Doctrine*, 35.
[41] Patient, *On the Doctrine*, 38.
[42] Patient, *On the Doctrine*, 39.
[43] Patient, *On the Doctrine*, 42.
[44] Patient, *On the Doctrine*, 43.

Covenant of Works

Contemporary Reformed and Covenant theologians understand that the Covenant of Works was a pre-Fall covenant, while all additional, less significant covenants are part of a larger Covenant of Grace. Thus, when Patient labels circumcision as a Covenant of Works it understandably sets off alarm bells for modern readers. However, we need to remember that this book was written in 1654, a period when many theological terms were still being established. For our ears, it might be better to understand Patient as placing circumcision in categories of an Old versus New Covenant. Patient is striving to show circumcision as a temporal and conditional covenant that is both distinct from baptism and inapplicable to a New Testament faith. Beginning on page 44 until page 70, Patient makes seven arguments.

First, he argues that circumcision is conditional and temporal. Using the Abrahamic Covenant of Genesis 17, Patient explains that the promise of land was conditional upon the Jewish people keeping the Law...including circumcision. Because circumcision was a conditional covenant, Patient concludes that it was "no covenant of life, but a covenant of works."[45] Second, Patient explains that circumcision is a Covenant of Works because it was a "National covenant"[46] only applying to the Jewish nation while the New Covenant applies to both Jews and Gentiles. He explains that Abraham and his Jewish descendants actually lived under two covenants: works and grace. Justification came via believing in the Covenant of Grace, "believing in the promise of the Messiah."[47] Patient

---

[45] Patient, *On the Doctrine*, 48.
[46] Patient, *On the Doctrine*, 48.
[47] Patient, *On the Doctrine*, 52.

explains that the Covenant of Circumcision "was of sealing use to Abraham, to confirm this other covenant, and a school-master to lead to Christ, as all other branches of that old covenant were."[48] Circumcision served to seal Abraham because it demonstrated his faith in the Covenant of Grace, and for his descendants, it was to be a sign pointing them to the Messiah. Third, he argues that circumcision is a Covenant of Works because "there is no promise of eternal life in it, but of temporal blessings in the Land of Canaan."[49] Fourth, Patient highlights that one could be circumcised and not be a believer or could perform circumcision and not be a true believer. Specifically, he argues that a slave could be brought into this Covenant of Circumcision without consenting or truly believing. He argues that a "man by laying out a little money, might have brought a Person into this Covenant."[50] Fifth, Patient argues that the Covenant of Circumcision was a Covenant of Works because there were men, specifically Lot, who was "commended to be a just and righteous man, and yet this covenant was never made to him."[51] There were also those who were circumcised yet were clearly not part of God's elect. Sixth, Patient makes the point that the Covenant of Circumcision could be broken, but it is "impossible that the New Covenant can be broken."[52] He writes that a soul covered by a true Covenant of Grace "cannot be divorced from the Lord."[53] Patient understood that there was a distinction between the nation of Israel and the elect of

---

[48] Patient, *On the Doctrine*, 53.
[49] Patient, *On the Doctrine*, 58.
[50] Patient, *On the Doctrine*, 60.
[51] Patient, *On the Doctrine*, 62.
[52] Patient, *On the Doctrine*, 65.
[53] Patient, *On the Doctrine*, 67.

God.[54] Seventh, and finally, he concludes that if circumcision were indeed a covenant leading to eternal life rather than a Covenant of Works, then it would "overthrow many fundamental points of Religion."[55] At this point in his argument, Patient begins to explain the Covenant of Grace, which makes up the fundamental points of the biblical religion.

Covenant of Grace

At this point in his text, Patient spent roughly 30 pages establishing the Covenant of Grace as in conflict with the Covenant of Circumcision as well as the doctrine of infant baptism. By placing paedobaptism in a Covenant of Works category, Patient concludes that it denies a "fundamental point of Religion."[56] Because he felt that he had established paedobaptism as a Covenant of Works, the first explains that it thus denies total depravity.[57] Second, if infant baptism is a Covenant of Works, then it shakes the stability of eternal life for the elect because it is breakable. Third, this would deny the necessity of a conversion experience and open "another door of entrance into the Covenant of Life."[58] Patient also notes the insufficiency of circumcision for salvation by explaining that Jesus called the circumcised to be converted. He also explains that

---

[54] Patient, *On the Doctrine*, 69. Patient writes, "Israel were never (all of them) so much visibly in the covenant of grace."

[55] Patient, *On the Doctrine*, 70.

[56] Patient, *On the Doctrine*, 70.

[57] Patient writes, "if the whole body of Israel were born adopted Sons and heirs of a covenant of life, born heirs of Justification, then they were never heirs of wrath, nor in a state of damnation, nor never proved nor charged under sin nor never all unrighteous." Patient, *On the Doctrine*, 72–73.

[58] Patient, *On the Doctrine*, 76.

infant baptism destroys the New Covenant because it abolishes the need for heart change. It also destroys justification by faith in Christ because "it doth hold out another way than by faith."[59] Infant baptism as a Covenant of Works destroys the matter and truth of the church. In Patient's eyes, the most disastrous outworking of embracing paedobaptism is that it denies eternal life through union with Christ. Tracing back to the covenants with Adam, Cain and Abel, Abraham, and Moses, Patient labels them as covenants of "Ceremonial obedience."[60] He places circumcision and infant baptism in that same category. Those covenants do not lead to eternal life. Unlike the New Covenant, those covenants were conditional and temporal. Those covenants were not for bringing eternal life, but to "point out to all the world, where they must look for and expect the Christ."[61] They were not where eternal life was found, but pointed to the one who would give eternal life. In the same way, Patient concludes that those who experience infant baptism are not ensured of the privileges of God's covenant people. The most important point that Patient was striving to make was "That there was never a Covenant of eternal life, made with any but with such as did and do believe, all along until Christ, not since."[62] Infants do not have faith, therefore, they cannot be candidates for the Covenant of Grace which leads to eternal life and thus should not be baptized. Before unpacking six relevant passages of Scriptures, Patient concludes,

---

[59] Patient, *On the Doctrine*, 80.
[60] Patient, *On the Doctrine*, 84.
[61] Patient, *On the Doctrine*, 88.
[62] Patient, *On the Doctrine*, 93.

"none but such as believe, are in a covenant of Grace, because without faith, it is impossible to please God."[63]

Scriptures Answered

Beginning on page 101 until page 168, Patient addresses six key passages of Scripture to prove his position for believer's baptism by immersion. He begins with Acts 2:39: "For the promise is for you and for your children and for all who are far off, everyone whom the Lord our God calls to himself." He notes that the promises are not for all people, or for children of the redeemed, but for those that God calls. Patient writes, "those that are predestined to have a covenant of life, and the blessing given in that covenant, are first called."[64] Children are in the same category as all other Jews and Gentiles in that they are potential recipients of the Covenant of Life, but God must call them first. They also must demonstrate faith before they can experience the Covenant of Life. He summarizes his position by saying:

> I leave to any intelligent man to consider, how greatly erroneous it is to affirm that the promise of the remission of sins belongs to the unbelieving and hardened children of the Jews, that God hath not, nor doth call. So that you may clearly see, that the truth lies in this text, that the promise is to no more of fathers nor children, nor those afar off but such as God by his especial grace doth call to be the Sons of God by faith."[65]

---

[63] Patient, *On the Doctrine*, 99.
[64] Patient, *On the Doctrine*, 102.
[65] Patient, *On the Doctrine*, 105.

Patient believed children, even children of believing parents, who have not yet experienced the call of God to salvation should not be baptized.

Next, he focuses on 1 Corinthians 7:14: "For the unbelieving husband is made holy because of his wife, and the unbelieving wife is made holy because of her husband. Otherwise, your children would be unclean, but as it is, they are holy." Patient focuses on the meaning of holiness, arguing that it does not always mean federal or covenant holiness. He explains that holiness could simply mean "separating or setting apart."[66] One type of holiness was seen in the nation of Israel, vessels of the Temple, and the priests. All or some of these might or might not have experienced the Covenant of Eternal Life. The second type of holiness "infuseth into the heart."[67] This type of holiness leads to eternal life because it is when "the heart of the inward man shall be purified through faith."[68] The salvation of the mother might in some way set apart the child from the world, but it does not infuse holiness into their heart. Faith remains the only way one experiences the Covenant of Eternal Life.

Third, Patient examines Romans 11:16–17: "If the dough offered as firstfruits is holy, so is the whole lump, and if the root is holy, so are the branches. But if some of the branches were broken off, and you, although a wild olive shoot, were grafted in among the others and now share in the nourishing root of the olive tree." He outlines the "usual exposition"[69] of this passage as the root equaling Abraham, the firstfruits equaling

---

[66] Patient, *On the Doctrine*, 106.
[67] Patient, *On the Doctrine*, 106.
[68] Patient, *On the Doctrine*, 106.
[69] Patient, *On the Doctrine*, 110.

Abraham, Isaac, and Jacob, and the branches equaling the ethnic Jewish nation of Israel. Patient explains grafting as, "the Jews through unbelief with their generation were broken off, and so also the Gentiles with their generation and seed are brought in."[70] Patient has a different interpretation. He agrees that the root was Abraham and the firstfruits were Abraham, Isaac, and Jacob, but he concludes that this means Abraham was both "begetting and working *Abraham*"[71] as well as "believing and faithful *Abraham*."[72] He argues "*Abraham* in a twofold Covenant,"[73] which he describes as "double sense holy."[74] Patient means the Abrahamic Covenant was both "spiritually holy"[75] as well as "legally holy."[76] His position is that Israel actually had two covenants. One was by works, which was external and national. The other was by grace, which was internal and not exclusive to Jews. Using Hebrews 8:13, Galatians 5:6, and Galatians 6:16, he concludes that Israel's national covenant was "standing no longer in force."[77] Patient believed the New Testament Church, even Gentiles, are grafted into the Covenant leading to eternal life. However, the New Testament Church is distinct from Israel in that they are not grafted into the Covenant by works, which are external and national. He believed that the Old Covenant has become obsolete. Thomas Patient, therefore, saw similarities as well as

---

[70] Patient, *On the Doctrine*, 110.
[71] Patient, *On the Doctrine*, 110.
[72] Patient, *On the Doctrine*, 110.
[73] Patient, *On the Doctrine*, 111.
[74] Patient, *On the Doctrine*, 111.
[75] Patient, *On the Doctrine*, 111.
[76] Patient, *On the Doctrine*, 111.
[77] Patient, *On the Doctrine*, 113.

distinctions between the people of God in the Old Testament and the people of God in the New Testament.

Fourth, Patient cites 1 Corinthians 10:1-3: "For I do not want you to be unaware, brothers, that our fathers were all under the cloud, and all passed through the sea, and all were baptized into Moses in the cloud and in the sea, and all ate the same spiritual food." He notes that this passage, and its reference to baptism, was a type pointing to something else. He explains:

> But beloved, the drift of the Apostle here is (as it is throughout the Scripture) to give out the mystery and substance, that shadows typed out to come, according to that in 2 Cor. 3. "We are not Ministers of the Letter, but of the Spirit," meaning, that the main thing which the Apostles did hold forth in their Ministry, when they had to do with types and shadows was, to set forth the substance or Spirit, or heavenly things that was pointed at, and so here.[78]

He reminds the reader about typology and its centrality to Christian ministry. Maybe the primary thing that preachers do is, yielding to the Holy Spirit, explain how things point to Christ. Patient gives examples of typology: "Moses type out Christ; the temporal Covenant, did type out the spiritual and heavenly covenant, and the temporal Israel did type out the spiritual *Israel*."[79] He also lists other types the Bible utilizes like bread and rest. However, circumcision is distinct from baptism because these types "belong only to the spiritual seed, in whom Christ has come already dwelling in their hearts by

---

[78] Patient, *On the Doctrine*, 120.
[79] Patient, *On the Doctrine*, 121.

faith."⁸⁰ He then returns to the importance of repenting and believing, noting that one did not have to repent and believe in order to be circumcised. In contrast with Old Testament circumcision, Patient explains, "But baptism is a confirmation of our regeneration already wrought in us, and our new birth, and our union with Jesus Christ by faith, and therefore belongs only to them, where this regeneration is."⁸¹ Not only did Patient highlight distinctions between the New Testament ordinance of baptism, but he also distinguished the New Testament ordinance of the Lord's Supper from Old Testament ordinances. He recognizes that some would object to his position by stating that there were Old Testament saints partaking of the Old Testament ordinances with "spiritual hearts."⁸² But, Patient responds with, "Duties performed from faith with an eye to Christ were then acceptable when performed, though ceremoniously, and such duties relating merely to the covenant of works."⁸³ He also points out, "Only I would have you observe, that the carnal Israelite was without faith capable to perform every ceremonial Law, required by the old covenant according to the express tenor thereof, as truly as the believer."⁸⁴ Patient concludes that if the Covenant of Life belongs to all believer's seed, then it would actually lead to universalism because we are all the seed of "believing Noah."⁸⁵

Fifth, Patient addresses Matthew 19:13-15: "Then children were brought to him that he might lay his hands on them and pray. The disciples rebuked the people, but Jesus said, 'Let

---

[80] Patient, *On the Doctrine*, 127.
[81] Patient, *On the Doctrine*, 128.
[82] Patient, *On the Doctrine*, 129.
[83] Patient, *On the Doctrine*, 129.
[84] Patient, *On the Doctrine*, 129-130.
[85] Patient, *On the Doctrine*, 132.

the little children come to me and do not hinder them, for to such belongs the kingdom of heaven.' And he laid his hand on them and went away." He begins by noting that these children were likely Jewish children, but we cannot be confident if those parents were "believers or wicked persons"[86] or part of the Covenant of Eternal Life. But then he addresses why the parents brought these children to Jesus. Patient argues they did not bring them to be baptized but to have Jesus bless them and pray for them. Next, he comments on the statement "for to such belongs the kingdom of heaven." Jesus said that they were not *in* the Kingdom of God, but that they are *of* the Kingdom of God. Patient believed the point of the story was not about baptizing children but to teach people to have child-like faith. He defines this type of faith as "such souls that are by God's grace, subdued and brought into a child-like frame of spirit."[87] He applies his point to the example of the pride of the disciples.[88] Patient explains this type of faith by stating, "A little babe we know in nature will trust his parents, so the new born babe will trust in Christ."[89] A common objection was then raised that infant baptism is not a covenant leading to eternal life but rather a "form of administration, that the Covenant of Grace was then administered in."[90] He responds by asking the question "was there no covenant made to Abraham's seed, but only an administration of a Covenant?"[91] He answers that circumcision

---

[86] Patient, *On the Doctrine*, 133.

[87] Patient, *On the Doctrine*, 135.

[88] "When the Disciples reasoned who should be greatest among them, Christ set a little child as a pattern of humility, innocency, and harmlessness." Patient, *On the Doctrine*, 136.

[89] Patient, *On the Doctrine*, 136.

[90] Patient, *On the Doctrine*, 137.

[91] Patient, *On the Doctrine*, 138.

was not an administration of a covenant but actually part of one of two covenants in the Old Testament. Circumcision was part of that lower covenant that did not lead to eternal life and was temporal. That obsolete covenant was a "shadow of the heavenly things"[92] to come.

Sixth, the Baptist pastor addresses the account of Sarah and Hagar in Galatians 4:21-31. Patient has thus far strongly advocated that in the Old Testament there were two distinct covenants living side-by-side. One was eternal and the other was temporal. The eternal covenant led to eternal life and was obtained through faith. The temporal is now obsolete and required obedience to experience the blessings of that covenant. Circumcision was part of the obsolete, temporal covenant, while believer's baptism is an outward sign of the New Covenant. In his analysis of Galatians 4, he begins by pointing out that, "there were two covenants is most evident."[93] He explains that Hagar represents a covenant born of the flesh and represents Mount Sinai. Hagar was of Ishmael and was a Covenant of Works. But, the covenant of Sarah represents a covenant born of promise and represents Jerusalem from above. Sarah was of Isaac and was a Covenant of Grace. Patient concludes:

> All which time the covenant of grace and the covenant of works both agree very well to be in God's house together, but at last, as the free-woman brought forth Isaac, so the covenant of Grace brings forth Christ Jesus, without strength of nature, by faith in a promise.[94]

---

[92] Patient, *On the Doctrine*, 139.
[93] Patient, *On the Doctrine*, 140.
[94] Patient, *On the Doctrine*, 142-143.

The point is that there was a time when two covenants existed within the same house, but now that the child has matured, they do not live in the house anymore. For Patient, this means that there should now be no mixed church of believers and unbelievers. He concludes, "Therefore it is plain from hence, that there were no carnal babes in that Church."[95]

Finally, Patient closes this section by briefly addressing three more passages. Utilizing Ezekiel 14:1-5 he argues that those advocating for infant baptism are creating an "idol in their hearts."[96] Commenting on Mark 7:7 and 7:13, Patient states that if this is an argument for paedobaptism, then it would "thereby make void and frustrate the Commandment of God; where Christ saith, 'Repent and be baptized every one of you.'"[97] Here he calls paedobaptism a "superstitious invention."[98] Finally, he uses 2 Chronicles 26:14-15 as an argument for how God seriously desires pure and holy worship, thus the paedobaptists must repent.

Before Patient moves on to positively state his Baptist ecclesiology, he spends about fifteen pages addressing three objections. First is the objection that if infant baptism is simply a tradition and the true baptism is by the Holy Spirit, then one does not really need water baptism. Patient's response is that if one receives baptism by the Holy Spirit, then that one should be obedient to the Holy Spirit's commands. He states, "Again, he doth not only simply baptize them, as a liberty that might be done or not done, but commands them to be baptized."[99]

---

[95] Patient, *On the Doctrine*, 144.
[96] Patient, *On the Doctrine*, 145.
[97] Patient, *On the Doctrine*, 146.
[98] Patient, *On the Doctrine*, 147.
[99] Patient, *On the Doctrine*, 158.

Second is an objection of tolerance. Some might object to Patient's position by recognizing that God has convicted the Baptists to practice the ordinance in this manner, but has not given themselves or others the same conviction. Once again, he returns to the call to obey but relies upon the power of the Holy Spirit in his answer. Patient writes, "Whence you may observe, that God's main drift in making his Covenant and giving his Spirit into the hearts of his people, is, that they may keep his Ordinances, and be able to walk in his ways."[100] His answer is that if someone is truly converted, then they have the power of the Holy Spirit giving them the ability and power and obligation to obey his Word. Third, Patient apparently faced some objections from people who agreed with the ordinance of believer's baptism and would "willingly walk with them and be baptized, were it not for their rigidness, in that they will not have Communion with any (though Godly) that are not baptized."[101] Patient answers that some are genuine, faithful believers, yet simply have the ignorance of the biblical teaching regarding baptism. He cites the examples of Cornelius, Peter, and Paul when they had genuine ignorance of the truth and how they handled being taught the truth. In all three of those cases, they faithfully repented and changed their view. Patient calls those who hold to infant baptism to give the Bible a fair hearing and then change their position upon learning the truth. He again cites the Great Commission as a call to obey all that Jesus commands; therefore, the redeemed are the ones who faithfully obey the Word. Patient concludes with the straightforward statement, "Therefore the way that Christ hath ordained, is, that souls should be joined or added to the Church by Faith and

---

[100] Patient, *On the Doctrine*, 161.
[101] Patient, *On the Doctrine*, 164.

Baptism, according to that word in 1 Cor. 12:13; 'we are all baptized by one Spirit into one body.'"[102]

Baptist Ecclesiology

Thomas Patient closes the final eleven pages of his text by making four theological points about his Baptist ecclesiology. First, he addresses his belief that the ordinance of baptism should only be administered once while the ordinance of the Lord's Supper ought to be administered often. Baptism serves to "confirm our regeneration"[103] and therefore should only be administered once. The Lord's Supper serves to aid the sanctification of the believer and therefore should be "received often."[104] Patient held the position that baptism should be administered after conversion and before the Lord's Supper. For Patient, these positions are not irrelevant theologizing, but rather an attempt to faithfully follow the teachings of the Scriptures. He closes this first point by stating:

> I do judge such a man that hath not a tender conscience in such cases, is in that much unlike Christ, and shews much carnality, because, as you have heard, God will have the honor to direct his people, both for the matter and manner of their worship, and order of his house.[105]

Second, Patient addresses the essentials for a biblical visible local church. After referencing Ephesians 4:3-4, he argues that the visible church should be made up of those who are

---

[102] Patient, *On the Doctrine*, 167.
[103] Patient, *On the Doctrine*, 168.
[104] Patient, *On the Doctrine*, 168.
[105] Patient, *On the Doctrine*, 169.

converted. The visible church should not be a mixture of believers and unbelievers. According to Patient, the visible church should be made up of those who have the "same glorious Inheritance."[106] He also explains, "it is an essential difference, inconsistent with Communion, that the members of one Church should own two Baptisms, the sprinkling of Infants, and dipping of Believers."[107] Patient believed a true church would side with the believer's baptism position. He also makes a case that the main purpose of a local visible church is to help one another obey all that Jesus has commanded. Thus, the "main end of Church fellowship and ministerial power is to destroy sin."[108] Patient explains that Jesus has given his Church the keys to not only doctrine but also church discipline. Patient believed in an orderly local church that included biblical practices of the ordinances which were vital to a church holding sound doctrine as well as living obedient lives.

Third, based on his previous arguments, Patient states that unbaptized persons should not be accepted into church membership. Essentially, Patient argues that if God commands something (in this case believer's baptism by immersion) yet one does not faithfully obey the command, then a local fellowship should not bring them into church membership. For Patient, the issue is total obedience to all that Christ has commanded. He then answers objections to this position. The first objection is that if someone was redeemed, then they have a "right in all the privileges in God's house."[109] Patient replies, "It is true, faith and repentance doth entitle a soul, but

---

[106] Patient, *On the Doctrine*, 169.
[107] Patient, *On the Doctrine*, 169.
[108] Patient, *On the Doctrine*, 171.
[109] Patient, *On the Doctrine*, 175.

repentance according to the Gospel is a change of the heart and a resolution to obey God in all his commandments."[110] Thomas Patient believed that just because someone was converted, it did not automatically mean a local church should let them into membership. He understood an unbaptized convert as not living in faithful obedience. This explanation leads to another reasonable objection to the Particular Baptist position. What if someone held to infant baptism in ignorance? Even if an individual does not know something to be a sin, the local church understands it to be sin; therefore, the local church should not allow them into fellowship. Third, some objected to Patient's insistence upon believer's baptism for church membership on the grounds that he was resting too much on the ordinance. The objection says that he should not rest upon that ordinance but should rest only on Christ. Patient responds:

> There is no sound ground for this objection from either our profession or practices; for we do profess salvation, justification and the spiritual welfare to be merely of the grace of God in Christ, and that by faith only; and that our obedience to Christ ought to be performed from a principle of regeneration and union with Christ by faith; and answerable in our practice in that we dare not put any soul on obedience but from that root.[111]

Fourth is a final plea to "observe the rules of Christ."[112] For all of Patient's perceived harshness, he makes this plea "in

---

[110] Patient, *On the Doctrine*, 175.
[111] Patient, *On the Doctrine*, 175.
[112] Patient, *On the Doctrine*, 177.

all tenderness."[113] Thomas Patient closes his work by calling the reader to "obey the word of God's command"[114] before citing the example of the Apostles from Philippians 2:12-15.[115] Patient's chief concern when debating his position on baptism was to work out his salvation with fear and trembling as he sought to be obedient to the Law of Christ.

Thomas Patient opens his book with urgency, citing John 9:4: "for the night cometh when no man can work."[116] His urgency is for followers of Christ to truly follow him to the degree of obeying all that Jesus commanded. According to Patient, ordering a church according to the Bible is foundational to the discipleship process. He understood that a biblically ordered church is one that embraces believer's baptism by immersion. Modern readers might judge Patient's tone as harsh or intolerant; but he felt a deep urgency for his generation, his position was in the minority, he was facing attacks for his minority position, and he sought genuine faithfulness to the Bible's teachings. Patient worked out his salvation with fear and trembling, and he accomplished his goal of writing a convincing case for the biblical doctrine of believer's baptism by immersion.

---

[113] Patient, *On the Doctrine*, 177.

[114] Patient, *On the Doctrine*, 179.

[115] "Philippians 2:12, 13, 14, 15: Wherefore my Beloved, as you have always obeyed, not as in my presence only, but now much more in my absence, work out your own salvation, with fear and trembling, for it is God that worketh in you to will and to do of his own good pleasure; Do all things without murmurings and disputings, that you may be blameless and harmless, the Sons of God without rebuke in the midst of a crooked and perverse nation, amongst whom you shine as Lights in the world." Patient, *On the Doctrine*, 179.

[116] Patient, *On the Doctrine*, 1.

Overview of *Caleb's Inheritance*

Edward Warren, a fellow soldier in Cromwell's Irish army, published *Caleb's Inheritance in Canaan: By Grace, not Works* in opposition to Patient's *On Baptism* in 1656. His father (Edward Warren Sr.) had been Dean of Ossory (later Dean of Kilkenney) and was trained at Trinity College in Dublin. Edward Warren Jr. rose to the rank of captain in Colonel Whalley's cavalry regiment[117] and later he became a major. He was actively involved in the Cromwellian cause in Ireland, yet his anti-government activities after the restoration of King Charles II led to his execution on July 15, 1663.[118] Warren's book is divided into 8 sections, and 20 chapters, over 126 pages.

Edward Warren did not share his story in the introduction like Patient did in his book, but rather attempted to rely on "God's word."[119] After a passionate and even mocking rebuke of Patient, Warren gives some reasons why he wrote his book. Warren notes Patient's prominence as well as the fact that baptism was a dominating discussion in Cromwellian Ireland. He did not want readers of Patient's book to think that there were no answers or only weak answers to Patient's arguments. He believed Patient "shamefully abused"[120] the Scriptures in his explanation and application. The Fifth Monarchy referenced in Daniel is also cited. Warren explains that division had ruined the first four monarchies and "Division and dissention are, but

---

[117] Crawford Gribben, *God's Irishmen* (Oxford: Oxford University Press, 2007), 95.

[118] Gribben, *God's Irishmen*, 95.

[119] Edward Warren, *Caleb's Inheritance in Canaan: By Grace, not Works. An Answer to a Book Entitled "The Doctrine of Baptism, and distinction of the Covenants," lately published, by Tho. Patient* (London: George Sawbridge, 1656), 2.

[120] Warren, *Caleb's Inheritance*, 5.

the Devil's bone of hatred and strife cast amongst Brethren."[121] Warren's book was a warning and a correction. Warren also believed that he was standing up for the next generation.[122] He opens with five chapters examining essential aspects of Patient's argument. Patient believed Matthew 28:19 spoke to the minister performing baptism, the mode of baptism, baptizing in the name of the Father, and the subject of baptism. Warren's first chapter is devoted to rebuking Patient's character as someone who never embraced the gospel and was destroying a foundational doctrine of the faith. Next, Warren criticizes his treatment of the four essentials of baptism found in Matthew 28:18. He condemns different aspects of Patient's arguments, primarily concluding that Patient's reading is too literal and wooden to the degree that no one would really qualify him as a minister. Warren also charges Patient with generally confusing grace and works. Furthermore, he jabs that if Patient can confuse the Covenant of Grace for a Covenant of Works, then he is no gospel minister. The third chapter addresses the manner of baptism. Warren explains, "thus when Christ tells them of their being Baptized with the spirit, it appears to be meant of the spirit's pouring out, so that from hence its evident, that *John's* baptism was by pouring out water, and not plunging into the water."[123]

Warren argues that both Jesus and the Eunuch of Acts 8:38-39 were not plunged down into the water, but the water

---

[121] Warren, *Caleb's Inheritance*, 5.

[122] "Fourthly, Because the standing for this truth, for the interest of Infant Church-seed in the covenant, is a sprig of generation work, as the holy Ghost witnesseth, Gen. 17:9 which yet is opposed by our dissenting friends, I have therefore used this Trowel with those in Nehemiah 4." Warren, *Caleb's Inheritance*, 3-4.

[123] Warren, *Caleb's Inheritance*, 9.

was poured out over them. Regarding the link between the Ark and baptism from 1 Peter 3:21, Warren explains that this figure breaks down for Patient because "the Ark was never under water, but always floating, and so the persons that were in the Ark; therefore if Baptism be a like figure, then it needs not going under water for a signification."[124] In the fourth chapter, Warren explains that it would have been impossible for those being baptized to give a statement of belief in the Trinity. The fifth chapter addresses the final argument of the four, but more thoroughly than the previous chapters. Unlike Patient, Warren argues that the subject of baptism is believers and their babies. Warren argues that Abraham's Covenant was opened up to all nations, and if the Jewish children were part of the Abrahamic Covenant, then "children of Believers are now also disciples, therefore fit subjects for Baptism."[125] Regarding the baptism of the jailer and his family in Acts 16, Warren argues that it was unreasonable to believe that only believing adults were baptized that day. In summary:

> We see the whole catalogue, or cloud of family-witnesses and examples, in Scripture, do give in their light and testimony to Abraham's infant-seed. And that when the Scripture speaks of households baptized, it is meant parents and children.[126]

Warren saw continuity between the two Testaments where Patient saw discontinuity.

Chapter six refutes Patient's case that infant baptism is idolatry (man's invention). Warren argues, "grace in the

---

[124] Warren, *Caleb's Inheritance*, 14.
[125] Warren, *Caleb's Inheritance*, 18.
[126] Warren, *Caleb's Inheritance*, 24.

Covenant being unchanged. Therefore, children still remain within Christ's kingdom."[127] He continues his personal attacks in this chapter by calling Patient "Master Patient"[128] and a "poor man"[129] and someone who does not handle the Word like a real minister. In short, he explains that Patient was stretching the "strings of Scripture, until they crack."[130] The personal attacks are thick in this chapter, but Warren does not thoroughly refute Patient's position, except for the claim for the continuity of the Covenant thus the inclusion of unbelieving children in the Covenant.

Warren's seventh chapter criticizes Patient's thesis about the two distinct Covenants. Warren defines a Covenant of Grace as "a gracious engagement betwixt God and his people upon Gospel terms, requiring duties from them, in promising mercy to them."[131] He understood the Abrahamic Covenant as a Covenant of Grace, but also a conditional covenant because it has both inward/spiritual aspects as well as outward/temporal aspects to the agreement. Warren explains that God only made two covenants with humanity. The first was by works, but was before the Fall. After the Fall, God gives humanity the second covenant which is by grace. Warren understood that all covenants after the Fall are by grace not by works. He explains that the blood of Jesus established a New Covenant, but it was "to the same kingdom"[132] as the Old Covenant "consecrated by the blood of bulls and goats."[133] Warren concludes that even

---

[127] Warren, *Caleb's Inheritance*, 26.
[128] Warren, *Caleb's Inheritance*, 27.
[129] Warren, *Caleb's Inheritance*, 27.
[130] Warren, *Caleb's Inheritance*, 27.
[131] Warren, *Caleb's Inheritance*, 28.
[132] Warren, *Caleb's Inheritance*, 32.
[133] Warren, *Caleb's Inheritance*, 32.

though the Abrahamic Covenant had conditional aspects, it was a Covenant of Grace because it was given after the Fall.

Warren's eighth chapter focuses on Patient's claim that circumcision is a temporary Covenant of Works rather than an everlasting Covenant of Grace. He explains that Patient's view is confusing because it is an argument that circumcision is everlasting, but only as long as the Law lasts. Warren's position is that circumcision is like all the other Old Testament Covenants of Grace in that they are not temporal but everlasting. He argues further, "Justification by faith was not given by circumcision, i.e. by the act done, neither is it now given by baptism, yet Justification was given in that Covenant of Grace which circumcision sealed, and so the elect did obtain it."[134] Warren also makes the point that the New Testament never claims circumcision is in opposition to justification or a Covenant of Works. He concludes, therefore, that Patient had made a great mistake because the "Law was no covenant of Works, nor is circumcision or any part of the Law opposed to Faith."[135]

Next, Warren devotes chapters nine and ten to answering a number of arguments made by Patient. Regarding the seal of Abraham's faith, Warren explains that it was not just a seal to Abraham or a seal as a "badge of honor to Abraham's Faith,"[136] but rather to all of Abraham's seed as part of God's Covenant oath. Warren also calls Patient a false prophet for proposing the seal was only for Abraham. Warren refutes Patient's claim that circumcision was not a promise of eternal life on the grounds that God was promising to be the God of those who were circumcised. Next, Warren explains the Abrahamic

---

[134] Warren, *Caleb's Inheritance*, 50.
[135] Warren, *Caleb's Inheritance*, 54.
[136] Warren, *Caleb's Inheritance*, 55.

Covenant had both external and spiritual parts. He leans on this interpretation when explaining that some could be part of the external covenant yet be damned.

Warren devotes chapters eleven, twelve, and thirteen to Patient's seven fundamentals. First, Warren makes a case for all those within the nation of Israel being adopted to glory. Second, he claims that those who were part of the Covenant of Grace yet fell away from the faith are still part of the covenant because "the covenant remains stable, and the same forever."[137] Third, Warren notes that the gospel was preached to Israel and circumcision was a "Type of the circumcision upon the heart."[138] Fourth, Warren maintains that the New Covenant has conditions—the condition of faith—but this did not make it a Covenant of Works. Fifth, he maintains that children of believers "have the right to the external part of the covenant of grace"[139] but not necessarily the inner spiritual conversion part of the covenant. Sixth, he explains the church built upon Christ and his gospel is made up of "believers and their seed"[140] just as Israel was made up of both. Seventh, in response to Patient's charge that ministers who teach that one can be part of "a covenant of life, without an in-being in Christ by faith"[141] are blinded, Warren simply claims that Patient is a false prophet.

Warren addresses a range of points and Scriptures from chapters fourteen to twenty. He devotes chapter fourteen to

---

[137] Warren, *Caleb's Inheritance*, 65.
[138] Warren, *Caleb's Inheritance*, 66.
[139] Warren, *Caleb's Inheritance*, 69.
[140] Warren, *Caleb's Inheritance*, 70.
[141] Warren, *Caleb's Inheritance*, 75.

advocating that the Covenant of Grace can include unbelievers. He writes:

> He that hath Christ hath life, he that hath not Christ hath not life; we say the same; but he that hath not Christ spiritually, may have a visible right to the covenant of Grace, as those hypocrites had, so often mentioned.[142]

Warren addresses Acts 2:39 and 1 Corinthians 7:14 in his fifteenth chapter. Regarding these verses, he explains that God is applying the Abrahamic Covenant to even Gentiles and showing "special privileges"[143] to children of the converted. In chapter sixteen, he argues that Patient made distinctions in the Abrahamic Covenant that were "not to be found in Scripture."[144]

Warren devotes the final four chapters of his work to commenting on Scriptures that Patient addresses in his book. He focuses on 1 Corinthians 10:1-3 in his seventeenth chapter. The primary point of this chapter was that the Old Testament people of God who were baptized with Moses were not baptized according to the flesh but according to the spirit. Warren argues that Paul's point was to parallel the Corinthian Christians with Old Testament Israel in order for them to see that God could bring down the same judgment. Warren's eighteenth chapter addresses Patient's comments regarding Jesus rebuking his disciples in Mark 10 for keeping little children from him. He concludes that the Baptists are also guilty of the disciples' offense because they do not baptize children. In his

---

[142] Warren, *Caleb's Inheritance*, 86.
[143] Warren, *Caleb's Inheritance*, 90.
[144] Warren, *Caleb's Inheritance*, 95.

nineteenth chapter he focuses the debate on Galatians 4:21 and Acts 13:45-46 as well as the topic of the administration of the Covenant of Grace. Warren's primary criticism is that Patient made the mistake of thinking "the covenant of grace hath no conditions."[145] He explains that God's role in the covenant is unconditional, but man's part is based on the condition of faithful obedience. Warren comments on a series of biblical passages in his twentieth and final chapter. He defends against Patient's charge that baptizing infants represents a form of idolatry. Warren also rebukes Patient's charge by arguing that it was Patient who set up an idol in his heart and was going against the vast majority of Christian thinking. Theological works from this period tended to manifest a harsh tone. Patient's book can be categorized as harsh at points. However, Warren ends his work with a combative and even condescending view of Thomas Patient. Warren concludes by referencing the kingdom of God from Matthew 21:43,[146] noting that the kingdom Jesus was referring to was "the Church of the Jews who had the laws and the Ordinances of worship amongst them; in which kingdom was included as subjects, men, woman, and children by virtue of God's covenant made with Abraham."[147] Next, he bridges from that Old Testament reality to its continuity in the New Testament. He argues that the kingdom in the New Testament "be the same for substance, with that which was taken away from the Jews; then must the infants of Church-believers, be also subjects of this

---

[145] Warren, *Caleb's Inheritance*, 110.
[146] "Therefore I tell you, the kingdom of God will be taken away from you and given to a people producing its fruits."
[147] Warren, *Caleb's Inheritance*, 122.

kingdom."[148] Warren's final chapter briefly addresses a range of Scriptures referenced by Patient. He opens his chapter responding to Patient's attack about paedobaptists' idolatry, but reverses the charge and states that indeed Patient is the one whose heart is "swelled with pride, though yet pretending a voluntary humility."[149] Warren also makes the brief case that the Old Testament Church of the Jews was a kingdom that included subjects of the children of believers and thus the New Testament Church of the Gentiles should include those same infants of believers. He summarizes his effort as proving Patient's charge against the paedobaptists as false and "the truth is cleared from the contempt and reproach cast upon it."[150]

In the end, Warren accomplishes his goal of providing the reader with a biblical response to Patient's arguments. The tone is exceedingly harsh (however reasonable for the era), yet remains true to his desire to focus primarily on the Scriptural arguments. His book is a consistent case for continuity between the rite of circumcision in the Old Testament with the rite of baptism in the New Testament.

Contrasting *On Baptism* & *Caleb's Inheritance*

There are some obvious contrasts between the two works. Patient's text is one of the earliest in the history of the world on the doctrine of believer's baptism. He thoroughly explains this doctrine. Warren's work was written in direct refutation of *On Baptism*. Warren explains the widely held paedobaptist position generally held by the Congregationalists, Presbyterians,

---

[148] Warren, *Caleb's Inheritance*, 122.
[149] Warren, *Caleb's Inheritance*, 118.
[150] Warren, *Caleb's Inheritance*, 126.

Anglicans, and most Independents. His is a defense of the doctrine as compared to the believer's baptism position.

As explained above, one of the primary points of conflict is their understanding of the nature of the Covenants. Covenant theology understands all Covenants following the Fall as Covenants of Grace. Thus, in all of the post-Fall Covenants, the obligations are only met with the aid of divine grace. Therefore, each of the Covenants following the Fall is a call for faith. Patient explains that some of the Old Testament Covenants were conditional and therefore Covenants of Works rather than Covenants of Grace. Warren rightly criticizes Patient on this point in his seventh chapter. The most charitable way to interpret Patient is that he uses sloppy and inaccurate language in this description. A more critical interpretation of Patient is that he held a wrong view of the Old Testament Covenants. Many of the Old Testament Covenants are indeed conditional, but this point does not mean they are in a category of Covenants of Works. Faithful adherence to these conditional Covenants still necessitates faith and grace. It was good and right that Warren was critical of Patient on this point.

Patient applies his reasoning to explain circumcision as a Covenant of Works. It was indeed a conditional covenant, but Patient uses poor verbiage and poor theology to categorize it as a Covenant of Works. Faith and grace were involved in this particular Old Testament Covenant. However, Warren never truly convinces the reader of the close link between circumcision and baptism. More accurately, Warren never even makes much of a case that baptism replaces circumcision. Warren assumes the continuity, yet never outlines a clear argument for the doctrine. His lack of persuasion on this point is one of the greatest weaknesses of his work. Patient is, of course, highlighting their distinction, but Warren never truly explains the reasoning for their continuity. Patient's interpretation is correct that baptism is a distinct covenant from circumcision on the grounds that it is only offered to those who repent and believe. Warren never convincingly refutes this point.

Patient and Warren both go amiss regarding how to interpret Acts 2:39: "For the promise is for you and for your children and for all who are far off, everyone whom the Lord our God calls to himself," as well as 1 Corinthians 7:14: "For the unbelieving husband is made holy because of his wife, and the unbelieving wife is made holy because of her husband. Otherwise your children would be unclean, but as it is, they are holy." Warren links Acts 2:39 with Paul's reference in Galatians 3 to Abraham's Covenant. Thus he concludes "That if it be Abraham's covenant, it must convey the blessings of the covenant to all within the covenant, that is, to the spiritual seed, spiritual blessings; to the temporal seed, external privileges only: but still by one covenant."[151] These assumptions are neither qualified nor found to be persuasive. Regarding Acts 2:39, Patient emphasizes that the verse includes the qualifier of one being "called" and thus is referring to those who have been genuinely converted.[152] Patient addresses 2 Corinthians 7:14 by explaining that God receives people into his covenant in two different ways.[153] One way is for those who might not necessarily believe yet experience separation from the world and the other is through genuine heart transformation. Thus, related, Patient argues that "holiness" in 2 Corinthians 7:14 does not necessarily equate to conversion. Warren simply argues that

---

[151] Warren, *Caleb's Inheritance*, 90.
[152] Patient, *On the Doctrine*, 101–102.
[153] Patient, *On the Doctrine*, 105–106.

Israel and the Church are synonymous as it relates to these two realities. He states that the Church, like Israel, is to be a separate people.[154] Neither of these verses speak of the salvation of children outside of repenting and believing in Christ's atoning work on the cross. The terms "far off" and "holy" are not necessarily speaking of conversion. The better interpretation is to understand these verses as speaking of the general blessing a child receives when growing up in the home of parents who are genuinely converted and communing with the Lord. When addressing the issue of Believer's versus infant baptism, it is understandable to engage these verses. However, these verses should not be forced into a theology of circumcision and baptism.

The two authors differ in their view of the household baptism in Acts 16. Patient believed that those being baptized, even the children, demonstrated genuine saving faith. However, Warren believed that there were individuals included in the household that did not demonstrate the saving faith yet were baptized. He argues that it would be "unreasonable" to think that those baptized as part of a household didn't include unbelieving children.[155] Unfortunately, I do not think Warren convinces the reader on this point. He assumes too much regarding the passage.

Both Patient and Warren make wrong interpretations regarding the relationship between Old Testament covenants with Israel and its relationship with the New Testament Church. Patient was correctly striving to preserve genuine conversion as the mark of true Christians. Warren was striving to ensure a link between Israel and the Church so as not to

---

[154] Warren, *Caleb's Inheritance*, 93.
[155] Warren, *Caleb's Inheritance*, 20.

establish a theology of two forms of salvation. However, Warren uses troubling verbiage when he says there is a "twofold Adoption, and therefore...A twofold Sonship...A twofold Sanctification...A twofold Justification."[156] Being born ethnically Jewish did not ensure conversion, thus in that sense, not all Israel were sons of God. Certainly, every ethnically Jewish person experienced external blessings of the Covenant, however not all of Israel experienced the Covenant "infuseth into the heart."[157]

Comparing *On Baptism* & *The First London Confession*

While serving as a pastor with Kiffen, Thomas Patient collaborated in the development of the *First London Confession* of 1644. He was one of fifteen pastors representing seven churches in London who officially signed the confession of faith. Thus, as expected, Patient's positions in *On Baptism* are consistent with the *First London Confession's* stance on believer's baptism. Patient is consistent with the doctrinal statement on the nature of the Church, candidates for baptism, the mode of baptism, and who is to administer baptism.

Article XXXIII defines the Church as visible, redeemed, and separated from the world. The separation from the world is made tangible through believer's baptism. Patient did not give much space in his book to the nature of the Church. However, he did reference Peter's sermon in Acts 2 in order to make the point, "it is the duty of every man that believes and repents, to be baptized."[158] This position is not specifically on the nature of the Church, yet displays an understanding that

---

[156] Warren, *Caleb's Inheritance*, 63.
[157] Patient, *On the Doctrine*, 106.
[158] Patient, *On the Doctrine*, 5.

entrance into the Church is through genuine faith in Christ. Thus, Patient is consistent with the *First London Confession* by holding to a baptistic view of the Church. He held that genuine conversion was the avenue into the true Church, which was evidenced by believer's baptism.

Regarding candidates for baptism, Article XXXIX explains that baptism should be performed only on those professing faith. Patient agrees with this position in *On Baptism*. He explains the subject of baptism by referencing the Great Commission of Matthew 28:19-20. Only those who are "taught and repentant"[159] should be baptized. Furthermore, Patient argues that it is the "duty of such as believed to offer themselves to be baptized."[160] Thus, consistent with the *First London Confession*, Patient understood the subject of baptism to be on one who was genuinely converted.

Article XL of the *First London Confession* explains the mode of baptism as "dipping or plunging the whole body."[161] The Confession recognizes the theological reasons for this mode as spiritually signifying the washing of the whole soul as well as the death and burial and resurrection of believers in Christ. Patient agrees that the manner of baptism should be by "drowning, overwhelming, or burying in water, and not by sprinkling of water."[162]

The *First London Confession* explains in Article XLI that only a "preaching disciple"[163] should administer baptism. Once again, Patient agrees with the Confession. In order to

---

[159] Patient, *On the Doctrine*, 17.
[160] Patient, *On the Doctrine*, 20.
[161] William L. Lumpkin, *Baptist Confessions of Faith* (Valley Forge, PA: Judson Press, 1969), 167.
[162] Patient, *On the Doctrine*, 6.
[163] Lumpkin, *Baptist Confessions*, 167.

qualify his position, he returns to the Great Commission. Patient explains that the one administering baptism should be the one who is teaching converts to observe all that Jesus has commanded.[164] Thus, Patient displays a theology of believer's baptism consistent with the *First London Confession* of 1644.

Comparing *On Baptism* & *Baptism Discovered Plainly*

John Norcott wrote *Baptism Discovered Plainly*, and William Kiffen republished a third edition of the booklet in 1694. Kiffen and Patient served together in London, and, as they both signed the *First London Baptist Confession* of 1644 they proved to be like-minded theologically. Kiffen outlived Patient by decades and this booklet was republished two years after Kiffen retired from the pastoral ministry and seven years before his death. Even though Patient's work was published 44 years earlier, there is a relational and theological link between Patient and Kiffen and this booklet that Kiffen republished. *Baptism Discovered Plainly* is only eleven short chapters and an appendix spanning a mere 62 pages.

Kiffen opens the third edition with a brief letter to the reader explaining that his desire is to "follow Christ fully"[165] as well as keep "close to the Scriptures"[166] as he addresses this matter of doctrine and worship. John Norcott's letter to the reader is listed after Kiffen's. The reader is challenged in the introduction to read this booklet "without prejudice."[167]

---

[164] Patient, *On the Doctrine*, 6.
[165] John Norcott, *Baptism Discovered Plainly & Faithfully According to the Word of God* (London: Norcott, 1694), A2.
[166] Norcott, *Baptism Discovered Plainly*, A3.
[167] Norcott, *Baptism Discovered Plainly*, 1.

ON BAPTISM

The first chapter explains that at Jesus' baptism he was immersed and it explains that he is our pattern. The second chapter assumes the Great Commission is a reference to believer's baptism. It explains the passage and argues that it should be every Christian's pattern. The next chapter examines eight instances of baptism, mostly from the book of Acts. These examples are shown to be baptisms by immersion and baptisms after the individual has professed "Faith and repentance; and were of years able to answer for themselves."[168] The fourth chapter has two sections. First is a basic case for believer's baptism by immersion. Norcott makes points such as referencing the fact that the Greek term *baptizo* means "to plunge, to overwhelm."[169] Highlighting immersion, he notes a Dutch version of the Bible that calls John "the Dipper"[170] as opposed to "the Baptizer." Norcott also explains that Romans 6:4 and Colossians 2:12 can only be understood through the lens of believer's baptism. In the second section, questions are raised and answered. One question is if there is really any virtue in simply the amount of water used in the rite. The question is answered emphatically because God has ordained the manner of this ordinance. He explains that the purpose of the ordinance is lost if one is sprinkled and it also goes against the biblical pattern. The fifth chapter makes the case that Christ instituted believer's baptism by immersion, but never repealed it, therefore it should still be practiced. The sixth chapter makes the point that there is no reason, either from grace or the Spirit, that a believer should not be baptized. The seventh chapter is set in opposition to those who desire to demean or diminish

---

[168] Norcott, *Baptism Discovered Plainly*, 11–12.
[169] Norcott, *Baptism Discovered Plainly*, 17.
[170] Norcott, *Baptism Discovered Plainly*, 17.

believer's baptism. This short two-page chapter advocates the greatness and significance of the ordinance.

The eighth chapter answers twenty-two objections to believer's baptism by immersion. Regarding the relevance of circumcision (and its related ordinance of paedobaptism), Norcott writes, "Now in the Gospel it is nothing, because abolished, Gal. 5:2. 'If you be circumcised, Christ shall profit you nothing.'"[171] He acknowledges that there is a Spirit baptism, and water baptism is a shadow, but then remarks, "yet consider Christ subjected to it, and who art thou, wilt thou be wiser than Christ?"[172] Regarding the question of a legitimate link between circumcision and infant baptism he states, "there's not any Word of God for such a thing, and thou must not be wise above what is written."[173] The question is posed about godly men who hold a different position, to which he responds that we are "not to follow an Apostle further than he followeth Christ."[174] Next, the objection is raised that there is no prohibition against baptizing infants, to which he responds that Nadab and Abihu faced the wrath of God for what they did even though there was not a particular prohibition. Regarding the apparent family baptisms, he highlights the verses that state that they first believed before they were baptized. Regarding the continuity of Abraham's seed, he says, "God did make a Covenant with Abraham and his natural Seed, to give them the Land of Canaan, Gen. 17:7, 8. but as to the Promise of Life and Salvation, this was made to Abraham and his spiritual Seed, Gal. 3:16."[175]

---

[171] Norcott, *Baptism Discovered Plainly*, 30.
[172] Norcott, *Baptism Discovered Plainly*, 31.
[173] Norcott, *Baptism Discovered Plainly*, 31.
[174] Norcott, *Baptism Discovered Plainly*, 32.
[175] Norcott, *Baptism Discovered Plainly*, 36.

In response to the "your children" reference in Acts 2:39, he encourages the reader to finish reading the verse. He emphasizes those who are called as the redeemed remnant. In reference to the holiness of the unbelieving children and spouses of believers, he explains that holiness does not necessarily mean an inherent or salvific holiness.

The ninth chapter is a table chart comparing the two opposing positions on baptism. Twenty-eight comparisons are made. Of course, the chart is biased toward the believer's baptism position, but the comparisons are also striking and convincing. For example, there are many examples of believers being baptized in the New Testament but none of infants, believers have faith and obedience and infants have neither, believers are converted while infants are not, and believers know Christ to be precious while infants do not. The tenth chapter is a listing of twenty-nine Scriptures that explain baptism "without any human consequence from man's wisdom."[176] The eleventh chapter is a listing of twenty-eight final considerations for those considering the validity of the doctrine. He calls his readers to consider that they "livest in the neglect of a great Gospel Ordinance"[177] if they will not be baptized after their conversion but rather appeal to the validity of their infant baptism. He also asks the reader to consider the clear examples found in the Scriptures regarding believers being baptized after their conversion experience. Finally, an appendix is included to address four more objections. He points the readers to Romans 9:6–8 for the answer regarding why infants of believers should not be baptized. Regarding the promises to Abraham's seed, he makes a distinction between Abraham's spiritual seed versus his

---

[176] Norcott, *Baptism Discovered Plainly*, 47.
[177] Norcott, *Baptism Discovered Plainly*, 51.

physical seed. Norcott also explains that some make a case for "Infused habit of believing, and that all the Infants of Believers have this infused habit."[178] Norcott dismisses this idea because the adherents cannot produce any Scriptures to support their claims. Finally, he states that infants do not have a seal of the Covenant of Grace.

The most notable distinction between *On Baptism* and *Baptism Discovered Plainly* is that Norcott's booklet is much more concise than Patient's book. He describes his work as a "Short and plain discourse."[179] Related, Norcott does not develop ideas to the degree of Patient's *On Baptism*. For example, Patient spends nearly 25 pages developing the idea that the Covenant of Circumcision was part of the Covenant of Works. Norcott addresses the relationship between circumcision and infant baptism but in a concise almost bullet-point manner. Norcott's booklet is more of a reference guide to the issue of believer's baptism. Patient spends considerable space arguing the links between the Covenant of Works and infant baptism. He advocates a position that those who hold to infant baptism are holding to a works-based salvation. Most contemporary readers, as well as Patient's contemporaries, would view this as a scandalous and harsh position. Norcott does not attack the other position in his *Baptism Discovered Plainly,* but rather he defends his own position. When Norcott raises the objection, "But are not very Godly men...that hold Infant baptism" he answers by advising the reader "not to follow an Apostle further than he followeth Christ."[180] This answer is much more charitable than Patient's questioning of his opponents' view of

---

[178] Norcott, *Baptism Discovered Plainly*, 59.
[179] Norcott, *Baptism Discovered Plainly*, A2.
[180] Norcott, *Baptism Discovered Plainly*, 32.

justification. Norcott also writes with more clarity on the issue of the Abrahamic Covenant and its relationship to his seeds. He correctly and succinctly writes, "The new Covenant promises were made to Abraham and his spiritual seed, that is, Believers; for they are the children of God, and heirs according to the promise."[181] Norcott makes a distinction between the physical and spiritual seeds of Abraham. Contemporary theologians make the same contrast. Finally, another distinction; Norcott did not address the issue of the authority of the baptizer.

However, both embrace a very high view of Scripture and argue their points primarily from the Bible. Both works list Scripture after Scripture to advance the believer's baptism position. Patient would agree with all of Norcott's positions. Both understood that Christ calls for baptism as part of discipleship after one is converted. Both understood that genuine faith should precede baptism. Both understood that baptism should be via immersion or dipping. Both understood that believer's baptism is a significant ordinance that should be seriously considered by every believer.

Summary of Patient's Baptismal Theology

Thomas Patient's theology of believer's baptism began with his theology of the Bible. As a signatory of the *First London Confession,* he understood the Bible as being "plainly revealed"[182] and as providing what we need to know regarding the "office of Christ, in whom all the promises are Yea and Amen."[183] His motives for writing his book about baptism was

---

[181] Norcott, *Baptism Discovered Plainly*, 58.
[182] Article VIII (Lumpkin, *Baptist Confessions*, 158).
[183] Article VIII (Lumpkin, *Baptist Confessions*, 158).

rooted in this commitment to the authority of the Bible. He opens his introduction with the urgent warning, "the night cometh,"[184] from John 9:4. Additionally, in his introduction, he explains that many people write books on theological topics "stuffed with very much of man's wisdom."[185] In contrast, Patient sought to stuff his book with "clear Scripture-evidence."[186] This logic demonstrates that his theology of believer's baptism is rooted in his commitment to the authority of the Bible.

His believer's baptism theology is also rooted in his understanding of how grace enables salvation and sanctification. Article V of the *First London Confession* reads:

> All mankind being thus fallen, and become altogether dead in sins and trespasses, and subject to the eternal wrath of the great God by transgression; yet the elect, which God hath loved with an everlasting love, are redeemed, quickened, and saved, not by themselves, neither by their own works, lest any man should boast himself, but wholly and only by God of His free grace and mercy through Jesus Christ, who of God is made unto us wisdom, righteousness, sanctification, and redemption, that as it is written, He that rejoiceth, let him rejoice in the Lord.[187]

Patient understood that both redemption and sanctification are enabled through the free grace of God. Furthermore, grace is the ground of one of his main arguments against paedobaptism. As mentioned above, Patient's language about the two

---

[184] Patient, *On the Doctrine*, A2.
[185] Patient, *On the Doctrine*, A3.
[186] Patient, *On the Doctrine*, A3.
[187] Article V (Lumpkin, *Baptist Confessions*, 158).

covenants is troublesome. He rightly understood Old versus New Covenants. However, he oversimplifies the Old Covenant as a Conditional Covenant as well as a Covenant of Works.[188] Even though most would disagree with his understanding of the Old Covenant, Patient's concern was grace. He saw parents baptizing their babies with the hope that their children would enter heaven. He saw those baptisms as a form of work's righteousness. Patient's theology of baptism is firmly rooted in his commitment to a gospel of grace versus works.

Thomas Patient's baptismal theology is also rooted in his related commitments to the Great Commission and a pure church made up of converted believers. Patient, like all of his Baptist contemporaries, looked at Matthew 18 as the ground for their Congregationalism. Citing Matthew 18:17, the *First London Confession* in Article XLII states, "Christ has likewise given power to His whole church to receive in and cast out."[189] Thus, it was imperative to the Baptists that those rendering judgment regarding the genuineness of someone's faith must indeed display genuine faith. Patient allowed the Great Commission to guide his thinking at this point. His commitment to the Great Commission led to his understanding that "believing the Gospel is to come before baptizing."[190] Thus, Patient had a commitment to see unbelievers convert into believers before their baptism. He desired a pure church of converted, then baptized, believers who had the ability to rightfully render judgment in a church discipline case according to Matthew 18.

---

[188] Patient writes, "Secondly, I shall prove, that the Covenant of Circumcision was no Covenant of eternal life, but a Conditional Covenant, a Covenant of Works." Patient, *On the Doctrine*, 28.

[189] Lumpkin, *Baptist Confessions*, 168.

[190] Patient, *On the Doctrine*, 17.

Patient's theology of believer's baptism was interwoven with his commitment to the Great Commission and a pure converted church.

The Great Commission is not solely a statement about evangelism and conversion, but is also about discipleship and maturing spiritually. Patient's theology of believer's baptism was also rooted in his commitment to Christian discipleship. Article XXXIX of the *London Confession* describes a disciple as one "professing faith"[191] in Christ and one who is "taught."[192] As it relates to baptism, the Confession states that the disciple "ought to be baptized."[193] Consistent with the Confession, Patient explains baptism as the "duty"[194] of disciples to be baptized. Thus, he believed believer's baptism was essential to the discipleship process as outlined in the Great Commission. For Thomas Patient, believer's baptism is a discipleship issue.

Finally, his theology of baptism was so significant that he believed it should establish new churches and even divide existing congregations. Patient established the first Baptist church in Ireland around the doctrine of believer's baptism. This work was in response to the sharp division that arose from this doctrine at Christ Church in Dublin. Additionally, Patient had been part of Kiffen's church in London, which united around the doctrine of believer's baptism. When he went to Ireland with Cromwell's army, his mission was to establish churches that held to his doctrine of baptism. Believer's baptism by immersion was not an irrelevant doctrine in Patient's

---

[191] Lumpkin, *Baptist Confessions*, 167.
[192] Lumpkin, *Baptist Confessions*, 167.
[193] Lumpkin, *Baptist Confessions*, 167.
[194] Patient, *On the Doctrine*, 20.

mind, but rather central to the spiritual growth of a convert as well as the establishment of churches.

In summary, Patient's theological convictions about baptism were rooted in other commitments about the authority of the Bible, a Calvinistic understanding of salvation and sanctification, the Great Commission's teachings about conversion and discipleship, as well as his ecclesiology. Obviously, he viewed believer's baptism as a significant doctrine. Further, it was a developed system rooted and connected to other convictions.

Conclusion

Later Ministry & Death

As explained above, Oliver Cromwell's son, Henry, was the ruling authority in Ireland beginning in 1655. Even though the Baptists had a rocky start with Henry Cromwell, by 1656 relationships were improving. The relationships continued to improve when Oliver Cromwell ultimately rejected the title of King on May 8, 1657. Baptists supported the title of Lord Protector over the title of King. Baptist leaders, including Thomas Patient, sent a letter of support to Oliver Cromwell upon this decision. In the letter they acknowledge the victories of the Civil War as great works of God. They also note how God reproves Kings. However, they speak glowingly of "your Highness"[1] but never refer to him as their King. Their supportive letter concludes:

> We shall only further add, that we do assure your Highness, that whatsoever report you have heard of either the Church baptized in Dublin or any other Church in ye same faith in Ireland. It is far from our

---

[1] Larry J. Kreitzer, *William Kiffen and his World (Part 2)* (Oxford: Centre for Baptist History and Heritage, Regent's Park College, 2012), 248.

> hearts to disown the Lords Authority in your Highness, or his work in your hand; but that you have with cordial and endeared affections been in our hearts, and the weight of your burden and work hath (by the prayers and tears (we can truly say) of the most unsatisfied brothers amongst us) been borne before the Lord and ye throne of his grace.[2]

Thus, the Baptists showed full support of Oliver Cromwell upon his final rejection of the title of King. No doubt the support of the Lord Protector improved the Baptist relationship with Henry Cromwell.

There is also evidence that Henry granted them greater religious freedom. Henry recorded in a letter dated October 22, 1658:

> I have since my return been more courted by The Anabapt[ists] then formerly, Mr. Patient and some others, who had not been with me of a long time before came to visit me, and expressed much as to their satisfaction with my management of things here, and yet their people had much liberty as they could desire, and much to the same.[3]

Patient ended his time in Ireland with a good relationship with Oliver and Henry Cromwell. Henry's mention of Patient in late 1658 is the last known reference to Thomas Patient in Ireland. Kreitzer concludes, "As best as can be determined he had returned to England by the spring of 1660."[4]

---

[2] Kreitzer, *William Kiffen and his World (Part 2)*, 249.
[3] Kreitzer, *William Kiffen and his World (Part 2)*, 208, 251.
[4] Kreitzer, *William Kiffen and his World (Part 2)*, 208.

CONCLUSION

Bristol

The Commonwealth began to fall apart in 1660. Charles II returned from the Hague and arrived in London on May 29, 1660. He was later formally crowned on April 23, 1661. Charles II's return marked the beginning of the period of British history known as the Restoration.

After Ireland, Patient eventually found his way to the Pithay Baptist Church in Bristol. This congregation could trace its roots to 1640 but likely was not formalized as a Baptist church until 1652.[5] While in Bristol, Patient served alongside the church's founding pastor Henry Hynam.[6] Patient remained in Bristol until 1664.

King Charles II's Parliament developed the Clarendon Code during the time of Patient's ministry in Bristol. The Clarendon Code describes a series of four Acts that had the goal of marginalizing Non-Conformists like Thomas Patient. The Corporation Act of 1661 excluded Non-Conformists from holding public office. The Act of Uniformity came down on Non-Conformist ministers in 1662. This Act of Parliament required submission to the *Book of Common Prayer* and led to the

---

[5] Latimar writes: "The earliest mention of a Baptist congregation in the city occurs in 1652. The members had separated from the dissenting body referred to at page 151, whose 'Records' not that 'divers of the church were baptised in a river'—probably the Froom...The Baptists worshipped in the Pithay, where they built the first Nonconformist chapel in Bristol, some remains of which are still standing." John Latimar, *The Annals of Bristol in the Seventeenth Century* (Bristol: William George Sons, 1900), 239.

[6] Ivimey reports, "Mr. Thomas Patient was settled here soon after the Restoration, but we have no information how long he continued. Mr. Henry Hynam, it is supposed, was the first pastor, how much earlier than 1656 does not appear." Joseph Ivimey, *A History of the English Baptists* (London, 1811), 2:541.

Great Ejection where over 2,000 clergymen were expelled from the Church of England. The Conventicle Act of 1664 forbade unauthorized worship. Finally, the Five Mile Act forbade Non-Conformist ministers from coming within five miles of their former churches. Later laws forbade the Non-Conformists from serving in the military and forbade them from attending Oxford or Cambridge Universities.

During this hostile environment, church records indicate that Patient was arrested on October 4, 1663.[7] Apparently, in violation of the Act of Uniformity and the Conventicle Act, court documents state he was indicted "for being at an unlawful assembly."[8] Patient claimed he was not guilty yet he also refused to follow the laws that violated his religious convictions. He remained imprisoned until the next spring.

London

Patient maintained his relationship with William Kiffen while in Ireland and Bristol. Together they wrote two pamphlets in 1660.[9] Furthermore, at some point after his release from jail in Bristol, he arrived back in London. It is likely that Patient was back in London by 1665. Kiffen was still pastoring what became the Devonshire Square Church during the 1660's. The

---

[7] Kreitzer, *William Kiffen and his World (Part 2)*, 252. The church book reads, "upon ye 4th day of October, Ano 1663, and put him in prison by Newgate. And one Mr Patience, a minister then in this city belonging to ye other Baptized Congregation."

[8] Kreitzer, *William Kiffen and his World (Part 2)*, 252.

[9] Kreitzer, *William Kiffen and his World (Part 2)*, 209. Kreitzer reports that they wrote in opposition to tithes a pamphlet titled *A Perfect Diurnall, or the Daily Proceedings in the Conventicle of the Phanatiques* as well as a satire about conventiclers titled *The Phanatick Intelligencer*.

minutes of the church book show that Thomas and Sarah Patient joined the Devonshire Square Church sometime in 1666.[10] Moreover, the church's minute book notes that Patient was "set apart as Elder"[11] on June 28, 1666. No doubt this was a joyful reunion for Patient. Kiffen was one of the key leaders of the Baptist movement and had a relationship since the early 1640s. Their partnership in gospel ministry spanned nearly 25 years. It was Kiffen's influence that sent Patient to Ireland and it was his influence that calmed the Irish Fifth Monarchy tendencies. Thomas and Sarah had been on quite a journey from the Devonshire Square Church to their Irish ministry to a Bristol jail. In 1666 he was once again serving as an associate pastor with Kiffen. This was Patient's station and church when he signed the *First London Confession*. Certainly, Thomas and Sarah Patient saw this stop in their journey as God's grace in their lives.

Death in London

Thomas Patient was installed as an Elder in the Devonshire Square Church in June of 1666, but only a month later he was dead. The church's minute book notes his death as July 29, 1666.[12] The report reads:

> Br[other] Thomas Patient who lately was ordained an Elder in this Church until 29th of this instant being ye Lords day discharged by death from ye work and upon his being then taken from ye evil to come and having rested from all his labours leaving a blessed savour behind him of his great usefullness and sober

---

[10] Kreitzer, *William Kiffen and his World (Part 2)*, 209.
[11] Kreitzer, *William Kiffen and his World (Part 2)*, 253.
[12] Kreitzer, *William Kiffen and his World (Part 2)*, 253.

conversation, this his sudden removal being looked upon to his own great advantage but the Churches sore lose. On this day he was carrried to his grave accompanied by ye members of this and other congregations in a Christian comely and descent manner.[13]

This record highlights the esteem the Baptist churches held for Thomas Patient. He had proven faithful as an English Puritan, an American colonialist, an English Baptist, an Army Chaplain, an Irish church planter, an associate pastor in Bristol, and then faithful again at the Devonshire Square Church. The London Baptists rightly honored Patient for his faithful service to the Lord.

The Great Plague raged in London throughout 1665 and 1666. Patient likely died of the plague during this particular crisis. The plague had the potential to quickly kill those infected. His death must have been sudden because he likely would not have been installed as an Elder if he was experiencing poor health. In addition to the historical account of the Great Plague, Krietzer notes a particular scourge during the summer of 1666 as well as a comment in the Devonshire Square Church minute book noting his death was during the "Time of ye Plague in London."[14]

Thomas Patient established a will after leaving Ireland upon the restoration of the English monarchy. His will was signed on September 29, 1661. He notes confidence in his salvation by writing, "I do give and bequeath my soul unto my God who hath assured me that he is my redeemer and my body to the earth from whence it came."[15] However, not much is

---

[13] Kreitzer, *William Kiffen and his World (Part 2)*, 253-254.
[14] Kreitzer, *William Kiffen and his World (Part 2)*, 209.
[15] Kreitzer, *William Kiffen and his World (Part 2)*, 254.

Conclusion

learned about his worldly wealth from his will because he only left his estate to his wife. The will was probated on August 22, 1666. More can be learned from Sarah Patient's will, which was signed on August 3, 1667. She left small amounts of money to relatives. Sarah also notes the existence of an "Estate in the Kingdom of Ireland."[16] She apparently maintained her relationship with Kiffen and the Devonshire Square Church after Thomas' death. Kiffen himself was one of the Executors of her will. Furthermore, the largest gift was to Hannah Halton, and Kreitzer traces her as part of Kiffen's church.[17] Sadly, Sarah Patient died in 1669, roughly two and a half years after the death of her husband. Her will was probated on January 18, 1669.

A brief phrase in the Devonshire Square minute book highlights the glorious side of Thomas Patient's death. When his life in this world ended, they simply wrote, "Died in ye faith."[18] The Lord had proved faithful to Patient and God's grace was made evident by Patient's lifetime of faithfulness to the gospel. To the end, Thomas Patient was a faithful brother.

Thomas Patient's Irish Baptist Identity

The best way to be remembered is to be first. Firsts are always significant because they launch something new that becomes the standard for the future. Thomas Patient was not seeking personal glory when he established the first Irish Baptist

---

[16] Kreitzer, *William Kiffen and his World (Part 2)*, 255.

[17] Kreitzer notes, "Halton and his wife, together with their two daughters, Hannah and Jane, were members of Kiffen's congregation." Kreitzer, *William Kiffen and his World (Part 2)*, 210.

[18] Larry J. Kreitzer, *William Kiffen and his World (Part 1)* (Oxford: Centre for Baptist History and Heritage, Regent's Park College, 2010), 183.

church, yet he became the father of the movement. His life and ministry are significant because it became the foundation for a church and a movement that continues even today. The historical fact that Patient planted the first Baptist church in Ireland is significant historically, religiously, and even ecclesiologically.

If one is studying the history of Cromwellian Ireland, then Thomas Patient should be addressed. Cromwellian Ireland is an important chapter in the hostile and complex relationship between Ireland and England. It was one of many attempts by England to influence and even dominate Ireland with their superior military might. The historical dynamics of Cromwellian Ireland enabled Patient's unique ministry. He could not have done this ministry in other places and in other time periods. For example, Cromwell's religious tolerance enabled the Non-Conformists to serve in his army but also serve as chaplains to his soldiers. Furthermore, the Cromwellian army allowed for this particular chaplain to expand his ministry beyond just the soldiers into the population at large. Patient's story is part of the broader Cromwellian Irish story. His life also fits within the history of the English Reformation. Politics and religious convictions merged in the history of English Reformation. Contemporary Americans tend to see politics and religion as distinct categories. However, the history of Patient's life and ministry highlights the inseparability of these categories in the English Reformation. Ireland has long been identified with Catholicism, yet its Baptist presence is traced back to this point in history where a civil war in England spilled over into Ireland, allowing the Protestant and Baptist message to spread throughout the nation. In other words, the Irish Baptist movement was birthed from the English Civil War. Patient and his ministry in

CONCLUSION

Ireland are by-products of these larger forces. Owen's sermon also highlights how the political reforms of the day led to religious reforms. It was Owen's sermon before Parliament that influenced Patient becoming an army chaplain and his ministry in Ireland.

Thomas Patient is also religiously significant. He played a role in the history of the English Civil War, which included a dynamic religious landscape. The English Civil War was an outgrowth of the English Reformation. Thus, it was not just a historical moment but also a distinctively religious moment. Patient was part of this religious fervor. He is significant in that he embraced the Puritan faith, even to the degree of traveling to America in order to find the freedom to practice his Puritan convictions. The Protestant Reformers were living out convictions grounded in the Bible. This led the Reformers to Calvinistic convictions about the gospel. These convictions were on display in the English Reformation with doctrinal statements like the Westminster Confession. Patient was caught up in this religious fervor and also sought to ground his religion on the Bible. These convictions led Patient to sign the incredibly significant *First London Confession*. The doctrines outlined in that early Baptist Confession became the doctrinal basis for his religious convictions in Ireland. As such, the *First London Confession* is linked to the Irish Baptist project through the life and ministry of Thomas Patient, and the Irish Baptist churches can trace their theological identity through Patient to this Confession.

Thomas Patient is also ecclesiologically significant. As of the year 2017, the Association of Baptist Churches in Ireland boasts 117 Baptist churches striving to minister to over 4.6 million people in Ireland. The church that splintered off Christ

Church under the leadership of Patient in the 1650's continues faithful ministry today! This church and this denomination can turn to Thomas Patient as the founder of the movement. Even though he did not stay long in Ireland, his work has continued for centuries. Remarkably, the Baptist convictions of believer's baptism and regenerate church membership remain convictions of this particular church and the denomination as a whole. If Irish Baptists want to explore the roots of their identity, Thomas Patient has left them a faithful testimony. Not only was the pastor behind the establishment of the first Irish Baptist church, and the first Irish Baptist church structure, but he also wrote one of the earliest books outlining the Baptist doctrine of baptism. While scholars and historians debate the meaning of being Baptist, the Irish Baptists have unique clarity on their origins and thus their identity. The historical record is clear as to the reasons for the split from Christ Church and John Rogers. Furthermore, the historical record is clear through the life and writings of Thomas Patient as to his Baptist convictions. It is also significant to note that Patient was a Non-Conformist Calvinist who held to regenerate church membership and believer's baptism. Irish Baptists might value religious liberty and soul competency, but these ideas were not the hallmarks of Thomas Patient's ministry. The historical record does not point to these ideas as having been the reasons for starting the first Irish Baptist congregation.

Evidence of Associational Partnership
Baptist identity is a complex discussion. Scholars and pastors debate what it truly means to be a Baptist. Moreover, Baptists themselves are a diverse body on a range of issues. This diversity is relevant for contemporary Baptists because it can affect

CONCLUSION

how Baptists operate and relate to each other. Brackney explains the problem when he says, "If Baptists disagree about their origins, they are equally disagreeable about what constitutes a Baptist."[19] Thomas Patient's ministry highlights the unarguable Baptist distinctive of associational partnership for mission and fellowship.

From the early years of the movement, Baptists were partnering together. W. T. Whitley explains, "from the beginning Baptists were not 'Independents;' they always sought for fellowship between the different churches, and they were very successful in arranging for permanent organization."[20] Their pattern was to organize into associations of like-minded churches in the same region. The purpose of these associations was to foster relational fellowship along with strategizing for evangelistic outreach.[21] Six General Baptists met in 1624 and 1630 to bring into fellowship a group of Mennonites.[22] Patient was part of the next major partnership of Baptist churches: seven London churches organized for the purpose of defending and defining their movement with the signing of the *First London Confession*.

Patient, of course, was a signatory of the *First London Confession*. This Confession was modeled heavily after the

---

[19] William Brackney, *The Baptists* (Westport, CT: Praeger, 1994), ix.

[20] W. T. Whitley, *A History of British Baptists* (London: Charles Griffin and Company, 1923), 53.

[21] Torbet explains, "Their purpose was framed by a desire to have fellowship between local churches and to carry on evangelistic work." Robert Torbet, *A History of the Baptists*, 3rd ed. (Valley Forge: Judson Press, 1963), 43.

[22] Torbet, *A History*, 44.

Separatist Confession of 1596. Article 38 of the Separatist Confession of 1596 reads:

> That though congregations be thus distinct and several bodies, every one as a compact city in itself, yet are they all to walk by one and the same rule, and by all means convenient to have the counsel and help one of another in all needful affairs of the Church, as members of one body in the common faith, under Christ their head.[23]

This article was used to create Article XLVII of the *First London Confession*. Thus, partnership was a hallmark of the mid-seventeenth-century Baptists along with their Separatist ancestors.

Patient embraced this concept of partnership. He was involved in the partnership of seven churches that related so closely together that they were able to develop a new confession of faith. The Confession was likely a defense against wrongful accusations against the movement.[24] However, the fact that they had common theology and established relationships enabled a partnership that produced the Confession. Furthermore, these relationships remained influential in Patient's life and ministry. Before his ministry in Ireland, he served as an assistant pastor under Kiffen in London. He returned to this post at the end of his ministry. The London churches did not

---

[23] Lumpkin, *Baptist Confessions*, 94.

[24] Lumpkin lists publications attacking the London Baptist churches and then concludes, "In order to distinguish themselves from both the General Baptists and the Anabaptist, the Calvinistic Baptists of London determined to prepare and publish a statement of their views." Lumpkin, *Baptist Confessions*, 145.

need to financially support Patient's ministry to Ireland because he also served as a chaplain in Cromwell's army. However, Kiffen was able to influence Patient and the Irish Baptists away from Fifth Monarchy thinking.

Patient was also involved in the early working out of this idea of associational partnerships as a broader strategy. Before the English Civil War, the Baptists only periodically organized for specific purposes. However, Torbet explains that as they watched Cromwell's New Model Army organize using county associations, they adopted the approach as an ongoing strategy. Torbet writes:

> The pattern of the more formal associational organization, as it has worked out, was provided by a military expedient with which Baptists had become familiar during the Civil Wars (1642–1649) between King and Parliament. During that first winter, counties were organized into "associations" for defense purposes. This plan was adapted to the raising of money and troops from the counties. Then Cromwell's New-Model Army, thus organized, brought into being a council for political action and protection of communities against plunder, to which each regiment sent representatives.[25]

B. R. White takes some issue with Torbet's leaning on the term "association" as a link to what became the Baptist structure of organizing in counties.[26] However, the Civil War played some

---

[25] Tobert, *A History of the Baptists*, 44.

[26] White writes, "But the actual word 'association' does not seem to have been much used among the Baptists even during the 1650s: they preferred to use the term 'General Meeting' for the periodic gatherings of their representatives or, as they normally termed

role in Baptists working together. The Baptist strategy of developing associations took cues from these early British efforts. Torbet explains that the strategy was firmly established in Ireland. He writes:

> In 1653 that part of the Army which was disbanded in Ireland, and which was largely composed of Baptists, transferred this plan to church organization as they sought to maintain fellowship between their lonely congregations in a strange country by correspondence and the frequent meetings of delegates. These Irish Associations sought contact with Welsh, Scotch, and English Baptists who were attempting a similar type of interchurch communication.[27]

Again, B. R. White takes some issue with these conclusions, largely on the grounds that the communications between the Irish Baptists and the others were not advocating associational partnership but rather suggesting a "monthly national fast day."[28] However, these communications do demonstrate a doctrinal and relational affinity between these churches. Furthermore, these efforts demonstrate a desire to partner for ministry. White correctly criticizes Torbet for connecting historical links that were likely not as firm as he believed. However, with that said, even from these early decades the Baptists were seeking to relate with one another and partner when necessary. Patient was part of interchurch efforts in London, was

---

them, 'messengers.' The Baptist Associations of the 1650s were regional far more than county in their constituency." White, *English Baptists of the Seventeenth Century* (Didcot, England: The Baptist Historical Society, 1996), 68.

[27] Torbet, *A History*, 44.
[28] White, *The English Baptists*, 68.

Conclusion

an important chaplain in Cromwell's army, and was one of the most influential of the Irish Baptist pastors; therefore, it is logical to conclude that he was central to these organizational efforts in Ireland.

Thus, Thomas Patient's ministry is a reminder that associational partnerships are a hallmark of the first Baptists. I would not argue that it is the one unifying Baptist distinctive, but I do argue that it was part of what it meant to be a Baptist during the first generation of Baptists. Historians only need to look at the life and ministry of Thomas Patient to see that the early Baptists were committed to partnering together for fellowship and ministry.

Early Full-Length Book on Believer's Baptism

Thomas Patient penned *On Baptism* in 1654 just after the close of the English Civil War. His book and ministry are significant because *On Baptism* marks a very early treatment of the doctrine of believer's baptism by immersion. Obviously, this doctrine is foundational to Baptist identity. Baptists view this doctrine as clearly taught in the Scriptures. However, during the time of the English Reformation, this was not a commonly held position. In fact, it could be argued that this doctrine was developed or established during this period in English history. Baptists rightly understand believer's baptism by immersion to be biblical. However, the majority of the Church throughout church history has not practiced the rite consistent with the Baptist understanding. Therefore, the doctrine of believer's baptism by immersion was developed over time. For example, McBeth reports 79 official public debates on the topic of believer's baptism held in England from 1641 to 1660.[29] The Particular Baptists also made their case and established their doctrine through written works. Thus, many pamphlets and books on the topic of believer's baptism from this period are significant.

Some Anabaptist and General Baptist works predate Patient's *On Baptism*. The General Baptists were more closely aligned with similar Arminian movements. However, Patient's movement was Calvinistic. He was part of the Particular Baptist camp, which sought to defend itself against the charge of being Anabaptist. Therefore, the Particular Baptists were not only defending believer's baptism by immersion, but they were also drawing distinctions from the Anabaptists. Many, such as Daniel Featley in his 1644 book entitled *The Dippers Dipt*, were critical of Baptists. Featley attacked the Baptists as "Anabaptists, heretics, mechanics, and illiterate men."[30] Thus, many of the pamphlets and books during the 1640s were defending the Particular Baptist churches against the charge of being Anabaptists. The clearest example of this defense is the *First London Confession*. The title of the Confession reads, "The Confession of Faith, of those Churches which are commonly (though falsely) called Anabaptists."[31] Additional examples of early Calvinistic works on believer's baptism include Christopher Blackwood's *The Storming of Antichrist, in His Two Last and Strongest Garrisons: of Compulsion of Conscience and Infants Baptism* in 1644 and *Apostolical Baptism* in 1646. Even though Patient's book might not be the first ever on the doctrine of

---

[29] Leon McBeth, *The Baptist Heritage: Four Centuries of Baptist Witness* (Nashville: B&H Academic, 1987), 64.

[30] McBeth, *The Baptist Heritage*, 80.

[31] Lumpkin, *Baptist Confessions*, 156.

CONCLUSION

believer's baptism, nor the only in his generation, it is significant because it is a thorough, full-length work by a leader in the first generation of Calvinistic Baptist churches. His contribution is part of a larger debate on the role and meaning of baptism. *On Baptism* is a thorough treatment of believer's baptism and is a defense against infant baptism. He outlines the goal of his work in his introduction when he writes:

> Christian reader, I judge the clear evidence of Scripture light, which I do hear give out to confirm the dipping of believers, will be sufficient to reprove all that darkness generally asserted in many large discourses, about this point of the christening of children.[32]

Since, as seen in this quotation, Patient's ministry was firmly Calvinistic and Baptistic, there is no doubt that the Irish Baptist movement hails from these convictions.

Religious Liberty & Soul Competency

Baptist identity is a hotly debated topic. Timothy George even identifies a "crisis in Baptist life today"[33] as the "crisis of identity rooted in a fundamental theological failure."[34] The debate centers on the question "What is a Baptist?" One Baptist theologian answered this question by stating, "As Baptists, our distinctive theological identity is an expression of our loyalty to Jesus Christ and His Word."[35] His reply is true, of course; but

---

[32] Patient, *On Baptist*, xiv.
[33] Timothy George, *Theologians of the Baptist Tradition* (Nashville, TN: B&H, 2001), 1.
[34] George, *Theologians*, 1.
[35] R. Stanton Norman, *The Baptist Way: Distinctives of a Baptist Church* (Nashville, TN: B&H, 2005), 184.

other denominations with different doctrines could make the same claim. The question about Baptist identity can be answered theologically and historically. A virtuous zeal for the Bible led some Baptists to reject creedalism, meaning they viewed humanly devised doctrinal statements as unequal to the Bible. However, this virtuous zeal led some of these Baptists to privatize their faith in a way that led them to boast of "their 'right' to believe anything they wanted."[36] Moreover, these Baptists claimed this right was the essence of what it meant to be Baptist. Some Baptists cite soul competency as the ultimate theological marker of what it means to be Baptist. Baptist's historical advocacy of religious liberty became one of the historical pillars of those advocating soul competency as the primary Baptist distinctive. Thomas Patient's life and theology add to the discussion about Baptist identity because of his early place in the history of the movement as well as his unique relationships with civil authorities.

E. Y. Mullins is a central theologian in the advocacy of soul competency as the theological Baptist distinctive. Mullins embraced the pragmatism and personalism of his day.[37] Mullins writes that personalism "takes the individual and personal life of man as its starting point, the highest datum possible for

---

[36] George, *Theologians*, 4.

[37] R. Albert Mohler explains: "Mullins also was influenced by his proximity to the faculties at John Hopkins University in Baltimore and Harvard in Boston as well as the Newton Theological Institute. Through these and other influences, Mullins began explorations in the writings of European theologians such as Friedrich Schleiermacher and Albrecht Ritschl. More directly, he was introduced to the pragmatism of William James at Harvard and the personalism of Borden Parker Browne at Boston University." R. Albert Mohler, "Introduction," in E. Y. Mullins, *The Axioms of Religion*, Library of Baptist Classics 5 (Nashville, TN: B&H, 1997), 8.

any form of philosophy."³⁸ To some it might seem like a subtle shift, but Mullins ultimately places the authority for truth on the individual human rather than upon divine revelation found in the Bible. He ended up affirming the Bible as true, but he also refused to claim the Bible as a revelation but rather as the "*record* of revelation."³⁹ In the end, Mullins found authority less on the Bible itself and more "on the autonomous individual and his or her religious experience."⁴⁰ These ideas laid the groundwork for his understanding and advocacy of soul competency. Mohler explains Mullins' idea as "each individual soul is independently competent to adjudicate all matters of religious importance."⁴¹ Humphreys defines soul competency as the "freedom, ability, and responsibility of each person to respond to God for herself or himself."⁴² Nettles describes followers of Mullins' ideology as the "soul-liberty party."⁴³ This camp answers the question of Baptist identity by claiming soul competency.

---

³⁸ E. Y. Mullins, "Pragmatism, Humanism, and Personalism: The New Philosophic Movement," *Review and Expositor* 5 (1908): 503.

³⁹ Mullins, *The Axioms*, 13.

⁴⁰ Mullins, *The Axioms*, 1.

⁴¹ Mullins, *The Axioms*, 15.

⁴² Taken from the chapter "Edgar Young Mullins" by Fisher Humphreys (George, *Theologians of the Baptist Tradition*, 187).

⁴³ Nettles links the conviction over soul competency with a rejection of objective doctrinal truth. He writes, "They view a serious confessionalism as contrary to Baptist witness because objectivity in doctrinal formulation tends to overpower subjective experience and individual perceptions of truth. Liberty of conscience, they key to Baptist life, cannot co-exist with the broad and objective doctrinal emphasis of confessions." Tom Nettles, *The Baptists: Key People Involved in Forming a Baptist Identity: Volume One, Beginnings in Britain* (Ross-shire, Scotland: Christian Focus, 2005), 13.

E. Y. Mullins went so far as to label soul competency as the "mother principle"[44] for Baptists. He states that the "sufficient statement of the historical significance of the Baptists is this: the competency of the soul in religion."[45] Mullins also taught the "biblical significance of the Baptists is the right of private interpretation and obedience to the Scriptures."[46] Thus, Mullins saw the idea of soul competency as *the* theological Baptist distinctive. Therefore, Mullins would explain Baptist identity as the movement grounded in soul competency.

Before comparing Mullins' view of Baptist identity with the ministry and theology of Thomas Patient, let us address religious liberty. All Baptist historians understand the historical role that Baptists have played in advocating for religious liberty and the separation of church and state. From the movement's earliest days, the Baptists were advocating for religious liberty. For example, Thomas Helwys (c. 1575–c. 1616) wrote *A Short Declaration of the Mistery of Iniquity* in 1612 advocating for religious liberty. It was sent to King James I, resulting in Helwys' imprisonment. Roger Williams in the 1640s was also famously advocating for a wall of separation between the "garden of the church" and the "wilderness of the world."[47] Baptist historian

---

[44] Mullins, *The Axioms*, 79.
[45] Mullins, *The Axioms*, 64.
[46] Mullins, *The Axioms*, 66.
[47] In 1644 Roger Williams wrote, "When they [the Church] have opened a gap in the hedge or wall of separation between the garden of the church and the wilderness of the world, God hath ever broke down the wall itself, removed the Candlestick, etc., and made His Garden a wilderness as it is this day. And that therefore if He will ever please to restore His garden and Paradise again, it must of necessity be walled in peculiarly unto Himself from the world, and all that be saved out of the world are to be transplanted out of the wilderness of the World." Roger Williams, "Mr. Cotton's Letter Lately

CONCLUSION

Tom Nettles states, "Baptists resist any intrusion of civil government into church affairs."[48] Walter Shurden is a more liberal Baptist historian who writes, "Baptistification is a *spirit* that pervades all of the Baptist principles or so-called Baptist distinctives. It is the spirit of freedom."[49] In fact, theologians in the vein of E. Y. Mullins established the primacy of soul competency on the historical significance religious liberty played in Baptist history. Even though Baptists' early convictions over religious liberty are a clue to the Baptist distinctive, it is an oversimplification to argue that religious liberty is *the* Baptist theological distinctive. Patient helps Baptist historians and theologians validate that claim.

Thomas Patient is helpful to all of these discussions on Baptist identity because he was such an early leader in the beginnings of the Particular Baptist movement. Furthermore, he is unique in his role of pioneering a new Baptist movement; thus, examining how he organized the Irish Baptist churches gives us a clue as to his understanding of what it meant to be a Baptist. Did Thomas Patient embrace soul competency? Did he embrace religious liberty? What was Patient's organizing principles when he planted the first Irish Baptist churches? Upon exploring these questions further, it will be shown that Thomas Patient assists historians and theologians to understand the Baptist distinctive is less about soul competency and religious liberty and more about the ecclesiological principle of regenerate church membership through believer's baptism.

Printed, Examined and Answered," in *The Complete Writings of Roger Williams* (New York: Russell & Russell Inc., 1963), 1:108.

[48] Nettles, *The Baptists*, 44–45.

[49] Walter B. Shurden, *The Baptist Identity: Four Fragile Freedoms* (Macon, GA: Smyth & Helwys, 1993), 2.

Did Thomas Patient hold to E. Y. Mullins' understanding of soul competency? If by soul competency one is referring to the genuineness of conversion, then, yes Thomas Patient rejected the idea of evangelism by force. In 1645 Roger Williams engaged in the debate over how to evangelize to the Native Americans. He wrote *Christenings Make Not Christians* where he makes the point that we should not seek the conversion of people by the sword of the government. Patient would agree, as evidenced by his understanding of his own conversion as a "change in my heart."[50] He further states, "true conversion begins with a prick in the heart."[51] However, Mullins and the soul competency camp are not speaking solely about conversion, but also about how to interpret the Bible and whether we can embrace it as objective truth. Rejecting the authority of Scripture is supported by this camp of Baptists in their rejection of creeds and even doctrinal statements on the grounds that they somehow violate someone's soul liberty. Patient embraced genuine personal conversion experiences from the heart, but he also embraced objective doctrinal truth—even to the degree of being one of the original signatories of the robust *First London Confession*. Article VII[52] of that Confession is not consistent with Mullins' position on soul competency. Even though Patient sought conversions from the heart, he did not teach people or organize the Irish Baptist churches around the

---

[50] Patient, *On the Doctrine*, A3.
[51] Patient, *On the Doctrine*, 4.
[52] "The Rule of this Knowledge, Faith, and Obedience, concerning the worship and service of God, and all other Christian duties, is not man's inventions, opinions, devices, laws, constitutions, or traditions unwritten whatsoever, but only the word of God contained in the Canonical Scriptures." Lumpkin, *Baptist Confessions*, 158.

Conclusion

idea that they had the freedom to believe or interpret the Bible as they saw fit. He understood that individuals, and churches made up of individuals, are not the standard of knowledge, faith, and obedience. Rather, he believed that the Word of God was the standard. Thomas Patient was a very early Baptist leader yet does not seem to have held to E. Y. Mullin's idea of soul competency.

Did Thomas Patient embrace religious liberty? Answering this question is more complex and likely disappointing to some contemporary Baptists. Patient did not fully work out his position on this issue, but he also did things that would seem at odds with our present understanding of the religious liberty issue. Roger Williams was a contemporary of Thomas Patient, yet Patient simply did not allot the space for the topic in the way that Williams did. No doubt Patient would have desired greater religious tolerance when he had to flee America and sat in an English jail as a result of his baptistic convictions, however, Patient also heeded the call of John Owen's sermon before Parliament that the government ought to fund pastors going into Ireland with the mission of converting the Irish. Contemporary Baptists need to clearly understand this aspect of Patient's ministry. Thomas Patient accepted government funds in order to plant Baptist churches! Furthermore, he sought to influence the Cromwellian Irish government not toward religious tolerance, but toward a more baptistic settlement.[53] Faced with a similar scenario, contemporary Baptists

---

[53] McBeth understands the distinction that most Baptists have advocated for religious liberty, yet not all Baptists have understood the issue or advocated for religious tolerance. Patient is one who did not advocate for religious tolerance when given the chance. McBeth writes, "A few Baptists, such as Blackwood and Tombes, taught a more limited concept of religious freedom, confirming Ivimey's

would no doubt do things differently than Thomas Patient. However, if one is attempting to claim religious liberty as the consistent historical identifier of the Baptist faith, then Thomas Patient is troubling for his or her theory.[54] He is an example of someone who was in a position to influence government officials and chose not to advocate for general religious liberty or tolerance, but rather used his influence to advance a Baptist religious settlement. This settlement did not come to pass in Ireland, but Patient unsuccessfully sought a sort of Baptist religious rule.[55] Again, all conservative as well as liberal Baptist historians and theologians see the virtues of religious liberty as well as the Baptists' righteous and courageous historical advocacy of religious liberty, however it is an oversimplification to argue that the essence of Baptist identity is religious

---

remark about English Baptists: 'Some of them confounded the power of the magistrate with the government of that kingdom which is not of this world.' However, these were exceptions which proved the rule. By far the majority of Baptists taught complete religious liberty for all." McBeth, *The Baptist Heritage*, 121–122.

[54] Mullins seems to claim that Baptists did not develop their understanding of religious liberty over time, but rather fully embraced it as an understood idea. However, based upon the fact that a leader like Thomas Patient did not develop the idea and advocate for religious liberty, it cannot be understood as a fully understood and embraced idea. Mullins writes, "There is no evidence that Baptists came to their view of soul freedom and separation of church and state gradually. There is nowhere a wavering note on this great theme. It seems to have been a divinely given prophetic insight into the meaning of the gospel and the implicit teaching of Scripture." Mullins, *The Axioms of Religion*, 60.

[55] Barnard quotes Henry Cromwell as concluding that even though the Baptists tried to influence leaders, they ultimately did not have a "spirit of government." T. C. Barnard, *Cromwellian Ireland: English Government and Reform in Ireland 1649–1660* (Oxford: Clarendon Press, 1975), 107.

CONCLUSION

liberty because someone like Thomas Patient did not organize a new and early Baptist movement around that idea, nor did he even advocate religious liberty to the government officials in his sphere of influence.

What, then, were Patient's organizing principles when he planted the first Irish Baptist churches? Answering this question helps Baptist theologians and historians more accurately answer the question of Baptist identity. If one wants to know what it means to be a Baptist, then one should look to what the early Baptists organized around. In Thomas Patient's case, the split he had with Christ Church in Dublin is the key to understanding his Baptist organizing principle. He felt that only professing believers in Christ should be baptized members of a local church. Thus, the doctrine of regenerate church membership as identified through believer's baptism was the issue that sparked the split in Christ Church and launched the Irish Baptist denomination. The organizing doctrines were not soul competency or religious liberty. Rather, Patient organized the first Irish Baptist church on a distinct ecclesiology. Therefore, Thomas Patient's life and ministry teach contemporary historians and theologians that regenerate church membership is the Baptist distinction. The pastors who wrote the *First London Confession* also organized their churches around regenerate church membership.[56] Regenerate church membership is also

---

[56] Article XXXIII of the *First London Confession* reads, "That Christ hath here on earth a spiritual Kingdom, which is the Church, which he hath purchased and redeemed to himself, as a peculiar inheritance: which Church, as it is visible to us, is a company of visible Saints, called and separated from the world, by the word and Spirit of God, to the visible profession of the faith of the Gospel, being baptized into that faith, and joined to the Lord, and each other, by mutual agreement, in the practical enjoyment of the Ordinances,

cited in the 1611 Amsterdam Statement.[57] What does it mean to be a Baptist? Thomas Patient would argue in the 1640s that it was someone who believed the objective teachings of the Bible regarding believer's baptism, which is grounded in the doctrine of regenerate church membership. Patient was advocating that only professing believers who had taken the step of being baptized as believers should become members of the church. Regenerate church membership was the organizing principle of the early Irish Baptist churches.

What role, then, does religious liberty play in Baptist identity? There is no doubt that the early Baptists advocated for religious liberty. Baptists were also the early proponents of religious liberty and further developed the idea. In fact, religious liberty should be understood as a natural, logical outworking of regenerate church membership because religious liberty, in the end, is freedom of conscience. Thus, Baptists should embrace our history of advocating for religious liberty and continue to work for it today. It is a central part of the history of the Baptist movement. Baptists have blessed the world in our advocacy of religious liberty. However, for accuracy's sake, Patient highlights that believer's baptism by immersion (grounded in regenerate church membership) takes precedent over religious liberty as the distinct Baptist doctrine.

---

commanded by Christ their head and King." Lumpkin, *Baptist Confessions*, 165.

[57] Article 10 of the 1611 Amsterdam Statement reads, "That the church of Christ is a company of faithful people (1 Cor. 1:2; Eph. 1:1), separated from the world by the word and Spirit of God (2 Cor. 6:17), being knit unto the Lord, and one unto another, by Baptism (1 Cor. 12:13). Upon their own confession of the faith (Acts 8:37) and sins (Matt. 3.6)." Lumpkin, *Baptist Confessions*, 119.

Concluding Word

Nettles argues, "Baptists must be Christian and Protestant evangelicals before they can be Baptist."[58] Patient is significant because his life and ministry serve Baptist historians and theologians who see the truth of Nettles' connections. Baptists are indeed first Christians, then Protestants, then evangelicals, and then Baptists. In the end, Thomas Patient was a faithful brother. Few, even among the Baptists, know his story. His story is of value to the contemporary church because he is part of a "great cloud of witnesses" (Hebrews 12:1) testifying to us that we can indeed, through the power of the Holy Spirit, "lay aside every weight, and sin which clings" (Hebrews 12:1) in order to experience the blessing of enduring towards our goal of "looking to Jesus" (Hebrew 12:2).

---

[58] Nettles, *The Baptists*, 13.

Appendix:
A Letter from Waterford[1]

The Church of Christ in Waterford, walking in the faith and order of the Gospel, do with all grace and peace to the Saints in Dublin.

Beloved Friends,
    We hearing that there were many of you that do not only believe, but have professedly put on the Lord Jesus Christ by Baptism, did think it our duty in the bowels of love to enquire of your estate; and we hear that you do not walk up orderly together, but are joined in fellowship with such as do fundamentally differ in judgement and practice; to wit, such as agree not with you about the true state of a visible Church, not the fundamental ordinances thereof. Now the Prophet saith, "Can two walk together except they are agreed?"[2] but that we may manifest to you, beloved, that we have a ground and occasion of grief, and offence at your so walking, as we shall make appear from clear sight of Scripture.

---

[1] John Rogers, *Ohel: A Tabernacle for the Sun: or Irenicum Evangelicum, An Idea of Church-Discipline* (London, 1653), 303-306.
[2] Amos 3:3.

Appendix: A Letter from Waterford

Consider the commission in that of Matthew 28:19-20 where Christ layeth down an order that is binding, which is this, "That they should teach all Nations baptizing them, teaching them to observe whatsoever by commanded them," (ye see here is an orderly way commended to teach to the nations). Secondly, to baptize such as are taught; and thirdly, to teach such as are baptized, to observe whatsoever Christ had commanded; that is, as we understand, all the laws of God's house, the baptized person is to submit unto, and by the ministers taught the observation of, and this order is binding.

And secondly, it appears the Apostles did so understand the commission, because they taught and practiced this order, and this only, to wit, first preached to conversion, then baptized.

Thirdly, put them in the practical observation of what Christ had commanded in, and to his Church.

Again, else the ordinance of the Supper would be prophaned, if that should be received before that fundamental ordinance, by which we put on Christ, and are ingrafted into Christ, and planted into his death. Now we say, this is a prophanation of God's ordinances, the Jews might as well be admitted such uncircumcised persons to eat of the Passover; but the very end of church-fellowship is the observation of all Christ's commands, as the commission holds forth; but this your practice, crosseth in that you agree to walk with such as have not, nor practice the ordinance of dipping Believers, and by your communion with them in Church-administrations, you are made guilty of their sin of disobedience, you willingly having communion with them in Church-administrations; for Beloved, you may upon the same principle admit, into fellowship one that will not receive the Lord's Supper, but pleads want of satisfaction of that to be his duty; another that will not own the ordinance of preaching, but confer only (as some such we know) and others that will not give alms, or contribute to the necessity of the saints; and thus in a word (upon the same ground) that you admit one that walks in disobedience to the ordinance of baptism, whither through ignorance or error, you may admit all manner of disobedience into your society upon the same ground, which is a total destroying, the end of Church-fellowship, which is to bring up every member to a visible subjection to all the Lawes of Christ their King, or else cast them out of that Society as old leaven.

Besides, in the fifth place, there cannot be true visible Church union without baptism, as appears [in] Ephesians 4 and beginning where the Apostles, pressing union, brings all these things essentials that must be agreed in, to make a people one, and that he takes for granted the Ephesians did agree in the same, which as he saith, "There is one hope, one Lord, one Faith, one Baptism, one God, and Father of all."[3] Now observe a true Church must of necessity agree in owning one and the same Lord; secondly, one and the same Spirit, one and the same baptism, one and the same Faith, without which they cannot walk together in the Lord. Again, many of these unbaptized persons do justify that idol of children's baptism, and consequently the Church and ministry from whence they had it: and you having communion with them, judge what you do, bring your selves into communion with, by entertaining persons into communion with you that are unbaptized.

Thus beseeching you to beware of by-paths, that our Lord and his ministers have left no footsteps for; but rather beloved, meet together, and lead one example of sweet communion

---

[3] Ephesians 4:5.

Appendix: A Letter from Waterford

distinct, using all means to convert such as have any fear of God, that they may come into you, through the door, and not at the window, as Christ faith is another case.

And thus leaving you to God and the word of his grace, that is able to build you up, we remain in the name, and in the behalf of the Church,
Yours in the Lord,

Tho. Patient.
Wil. Burgis.
Ed. Hutchinson
Ed. Marshal.
Rich. Sutton.
James Standish.
Swads.
Tho. Brenton.
Peter Row.
Wit. Leigh.
Geo. Cawdron.
Rich. Ladbrooke.
Edw. Roberts.

Dated at Waterford, January 14, 1651.

Bibliography

Barnard, T.C. *Cromwellian Ireland: English Government and Reform in Ireland 1649 to 1660.* Oxford: Clarendon Press, 1975.

Bebbington, David W. *Baptists Through the Centuries: A History of a Global People.* Waco, Texas: Baylor University Press, 2010.

Bell, Mark R. *Apocalypse How?: Baptist Movements during the English Reformation.* Macon, Georgia: Mercer University Press, 2000.

Birch, Thomas. *A Collection of the State Papers of John Thurloe, esq.* London, 1742, Volume V.

Brackney, William. *The Baptists.* Westport, CT: Praeger, 1994.

Brown, Louise Fargo. *The Political Activities of the Baptists and Fifth Monarchy Men in England During the Interregnum.* Oxford: Oxford University Press, 1912.

Claxton, Laurence. *The Lost Sheep Found.* London, 1660.

Coffey, John and Lim, Paul C. H. eds. *The Cambridge Companion to Puritanism.* Cambridge: Cambridge University Press, 2008.

Crosby, Thomas. *A History of the English Baptists, from the Reformation to the Beginning of the Reign of King George I.* London: John Robinson, 1740, Volume III.

Gribben, Crawford. *God's Irishmen.* Oxford: Oxford University Press, 2007, Oxford Studies in Historical Theology.

Dunlup, Robert. "Dublin Baptists from 1650 Onwards" *Irish Baptist Historical Society Journal,* V21, 1988/89, 6.

George, Timothy. *Theologians of the Baptist Tradition*. Nashville: B&H, 2001.

Grosvenor Baptist Church. "About Us." http://www.grosvenorbaptist.org/about/ (accessed August 1, 2017).

Haykin, Michael A.G. *Kiffin, Knollys and Keach: Rediscovering Our English Baptist Heritage*. Peterborough, Canada: H&E Publishing, 2019.

Herlihy, Kevin, ed. *The Irish Dissenting Tradition, 1650-1750*. Dublin: Four Courts Press, 1995.

House of Commons Journal, volume 6, 8 March 1649.

Howard, Luke. *A Looking Glass for Baptists: Being a Short Narrative of their Root and Rice in Kent*, 1672.

Ivimey, Joseph. *A History of the English Baptists*. London, 1811, vol. 2.

Kiffin, William. *The Confession of faith of those churches which are commonly (though falsly) called Anabaptists*. Aldersgate-streete, London: Matthew Simmons, 1644.

Kreitzer, Larry J. *William Kiffen and his World (Part 1)*. Oxford: Centre for Baptist History and Heritage, Regent's Park College, 2010.

Kreitzer, Larry J. *William Kiffen and his World (Part 2)*. Oxford: Centre for Baptist History and Heritage, Regent's Park College, 2012.

Latimer, John. *The Annals of Bristol in the Seventeenth Century*. Bristol: William George Sons, 1900.

Lee, Sidney, ed. *Dictionary of National Biography*, Vol. 44. London: Smith, Elder, & Co., 1895.

Lumpkin, William L. *Baptist Confessions of Faith*. Valley Forge, PA: Judson Press, 1969.

McBeth, H. Leon. *The Baptist Heritage: Four Centuries of Baptist Witness*. Nashville: B&H Academic, 1987.

Mullins, E. Y. *The Axioms of Religion*. Nashville: Broadman and Holman, 1997, Timothy and Denise George, editors, The Library of Baptist Classics: Volume 5.

Mullins, E. Y. "Pragmatism, Humanism, and Personalism – The New Philosophic Movement." *Review and Expositor* 5, 1908.

Nettles, Tom. *The Baptists: Key People Involved in Forming a Baptist Identity: Volume One, Beginnings in Britain*. Ross-shire, Scotland: Christian Focus Publications, 2005.

Norcott, John. *Baptism discovered plainly & faithfully according to the word of God*. London: Norcott, 1694.

Norman, R. Stanton. *The Baptist Way: Distinctives of a Baptist Church*. Nashville: B&H, 2005.

Owen, John. *The Works of John Owen*. Carlisle, PA: Banner of Truth Trust, 2000, vol. 10.

Patient, Thomas. *On The Doctrine of Baptism, And the Distinction of the Covenants*. London: Henry Hills, 1654.

Records and Files of the Quarterly Court of Essex County Massachusetts. Volume 1 1636-1656, Salem, Massachusetts: Essex Institute, 1911.

Rogers, John. *Ohel: A Tabernacle for the Sun: or Irenicum Evangelicum, An Idea of Church-Discipline*. London: Grey-Hound in Paul's Churchyard, 1653.

The National Archives. "Great Plague of 1665-1666." http://www.nationalarchives.gov.uk/education/lesson49.htm (accessed April 1, 2013).

Russell, Thomas, ed. *The Works of John Owen, D.D.* vol 1. London: Printed for Richard Baynes, 1826.

Shurden, Walter B. *The Baptist Identity: Four Fragile Freedoms.* Macon, Georgia: Smyth & Helwys, 1993.

Simpson, Alan. *Puritanism in Old and New England.* Chicago: The University of Chicago Press, 1955.

Thomson, Andrew. *Life of Owen.* Carlisle, PA: Banner of Truth Trust, 1965, *Works of John Owen* Vol 1, XLII.

Torbet, Robert G. *A History of the Baptists*, Third Edition. Valley Forge: Judson Press, 1963.

Underhill, E. B. ed., *Confessions of Faith, and other Public Documents, Illustrative of the History of the Baptist Churches of England in the 17th Century.* London: The Hanserd Knollys Society, 1854.

Ware, James. *The Hunting of the Romish Fox and the Quenching of Sectarian Firebrands.* (Dublin) 1683.

Warren, Edward. *Caleb's Inheritance in Canaan: By Grace, not Works. An Answer to a Book Entitled "The Doctrine of Baptism, and distinction of the Covenants," lately published, by Tho. Patient.* London: printed by George Sawbridge, 1656.

Waterford Baptist Church. "About Us." http://waterfordbaptist.ie/about/about.html (accessed August 1, 2017).

White, B. R. *The English Baptists of the Seventeenth Century.* Didcot, England: The Baptist Historical Society, 1996.

White, B. R. "Thomas Patient in England and Ireland," *Irish Baptist Historical Society Journal*, Volume 2, 1969/1970.

White, B. R. "The Organization of the Particular Baptists 1644-1666," *Journal of Ecclesiastical History*, October, 1966.

Whitley, W. T. *A History of British Baptists*. London: Charles Griffin and Company, 1923.

Williams, Roger. "Mr. Cotton's Letter Lately Printed, Examined and Answered," *The Complete Writings of Roger Williams*. New York: Russell & Russell Inc., 1963, Vol. 1, 108.

Subject Index

A

A True Confession. See
   Confession of 1596
Act of Uniformity, ii, 144, 145
America, xv, xvi, xviii, xxiii,
   xxv, 1, 3, 6, 52, 106, 108,
   109, 122, 123
Anabaptist, 11, 29, 30, 31, 32,
   78, 156, 160, 161
Anabaptist Rebellion, 29
Associations, 25, 34, 67, 71

B

Baptism
Believer's baptism, iv, 3, 7, 8,
   11, 13, 14, 15, 17, 20, 22,
   28, 31, 34, 36, 55, 62, 63,
   64, 66, 76, 77, 79, 81, 82,
   83, 92, 100, 102, 105, 106,
   108, 120, 125, 127, 128,
   129, 131, 133, 134, 135,
   137, 138, 139, 153, 159,
   160, 161, 168, 172, 174
By dipping 17, 22, 29, 56, 80, 105, 126,
   134, 162
By immersion, 22, 28, 55
By plunging 17, 29, 111,
   126
By sprinkling, 21, 22, 29,
   56, 80, 105, 126, 134, 162
Infant baptism, 21, 59, 62,
   78, 83, 89, 90, 91, 99, 101,
   102, 103, 106, 112, 123,
   130, 132 133, 162
Of the Spirit, 61
Paedobaptism, 7, 13, 82,
   83, 89, 90, 91, 101, 130,
   136
Baptist
American Baptist, 3, 12
Associations, 28, 154
Calvinistic Baptist, 1, 11,
   12, 15, 23, 161
Calvinistic Baptists, 27
Ecclesiology, 2, 76, 101,
   103
Education, 19
English Particular Baptist,
   iv, 3, 14

General Baptists, 16, 36,
155, 156, 160
Irish Baptists, iv, 18, 19, 26,
34, 35, 49, 54, 57, 67, 68,
70, 71, 72, 152, 153, 156,
158, 167, 168, 169, 172,
173
London Baptists, 18, 35, 49,
67, 156
Modern Baptist movement,
2
Particular Baptist, i, 15, 16,
17, 18, 21, 23, 24, 25, 34,
35, 56, 59, 61, 63, 67, 75,
106, 160, 161, 167
9, 61, 75, 160, 180
Southern Baptist
Convention, 1
Barebones Parliament, 68
Birch, Thomas, 49
Blackwood, Christopher, 6, 66,
161, 170
Book of Common Prayer, 144
Bristol, ii, 143, 144, 145, 147,
177

C

Calvinism, 30
Cambridge, 20
Catholic, 44, 45
Charles I, 40, 42
Charles II, 40, 41, 48, 143
Christ Church, 2
Christ Church Cathedral, 63
Christ Church in Dublin, 55, 59
Church and state, 32
Church discipline, 18, 105, 137

Church membership, 7, 18,
105, 153, 168, 172, 173,
174
Church of England, 9, 10, 12,
15, 19, 25, 77, 144
Circumcision, 85, 86, 87, 88,
89, 91, 96, 99, 100, 114,
115, 120, 121, 123, 130,
133
Clarendon Code, ii, 144
Closed-communion, 61, 62
Confession of 1596, 27, 30, 33,
155
Congregationalism, 31, 34
Congregationalists, 7, 11, 12,
31, 33, 46, 64, 69, 77, 120,
154
Conventicle Act, ii, 144, 145
Conversion, 10, 11, 36, 57, 77,
79, 81, 82, 90, 102, 104,
106, 116, 117, 122, 123,
124, 125, 126, 131, 132,
134, 137, 138, 139, 168
Covenant, 76
Abrahamic Covenant, 86,
95, 111, 113, 115, 117, 118,
133
Ceremonial obedience, 91
Covenant of circumcision,
85, 87, 88, 89, 132, 136
Covenant of eternal Life,
94, 98
Covenant of grace, 76, 83,
84, 85, 86, 87, 88, 89, 91,
92, 99, 100, 110, 113, 114,
115, 116, 118, 120, 132
Covenant of life, 83, 84, 85,
87, 90, 92, 98

Covenant of works, 76, 83, 84, 85, 86, 87, 88, 89, 90, 97, 100, 110, 114, 116, 120, 121, 133, 136
Covenant theology, 86
New Covenant, 84, 85, 86, 87, 88, 90, 91, 100, 116, 133
Sign of the covenant, 87
Cromwell, Bridget, 46, 53
Cromwell, Henry, 44, 48, 49, 50, 51, 53, 141, 142, 143
Cromwell, Oliver, ii, 26, 35, 40, 41, 42, 44, 45, 46, 47, 48, 50, 51, 52, 53, 54, 62, 64, 68, 69, 72, 108, 139, 141, 142, 143, 150, 156, 157, 159, 171
Occupation of Ireland, 1

D

Devonshire Square Church, i, ii, 1, 8, 11, 16, 22, 23, 40, 146, 147, 148, 149
Drogheda, 44, 45
Dublin, iii, ii, 6, 43, 45, 46, 47, 55, 56, 59, 60, 61, 63, 64, 65, 66, 67, 72, 108, 138, 141, 172, 176, 177, 179

E

Edward VI, 39
Elfreth, Mark, 36
Elizabeth I, 9, 39
English Civil War, i, 39, 41, 151, 156, 159
Enlightenment, 39, 40

F

Faith and repentance, 81, 84, 97, 106, 128
Featley, Daniel, 25
Fifth Monarchy Movement, 26, 47, 50, 69, 72
First London Confession, i, 1, 11, 14, 16, 17, 18, 19, 23, 27, 28, 29, 33, 35, 124, 125, 126, 134, 135, 137, 146, 152, 155, 161, 169, 172, 173
Five Mile Act, 144
Fleetwood, Charles, 44, 45, 46, 47, 48, 51, 52

G

Gentiles, 87, 92, 94, 95, 117, 119
Germany, 78
Great Commission, 59, 61, 79, 81, 103, 126, 127, 128, 137, 138, 139
Great Ejection, 144
Great Migration, 13
Great Plague, 5, 148, 179
Grosvenor Road Baptist Church, 66

H

Henry VIII, 39
Holiness, 93, 95
Holy Spirit, 2, 96, 102, 175
Howard, Anne. *See* Stevens, Anne
Howard, Luke, 35, 36
Hynam, Henry, 144

I

Independents. *See*
    Congregationalists
Ireton, Bridget. *See* Cromwell,
    Bridget
Ireton, Henry, 45, 46, 53
Irish Baptist church, 50, 150,
    153, 172
Israel, 84, 89, 90, 93, 94, 95,
    96, 115, 117, 123, 124

J

Jacob, Henry, 15
Jacob-Lathrop-Jessey church,
    15, 16, 17, 22
Jews, 87, 92, 93, 94, 95, 118
Jones, John, 62
Justification by faith, 9, 90

K

Kiffen, William, i, 1, 2, 5, 8, 12,
    14, 16, 18, 20, 21, 22, 23,
    24, 25, 26, 27, 35, 36, 40,
    50, 51, 52, 53, 54, 60, 61,
    62, 64, 66, 67, 70, 71, 72,
    75, 124, 127, 128, 139, 141,
    142, 143, 145, 146, 147,
    148, 149, 156, 177
Kiffin Manuscript, 21
Kilkenny, 51, 52, 54, 57, 63
King Charles II, 24, 42, 109,
    144
King Henry VIII, 9
Kingdom of God, 98
Knollys, Hanserd, 2, 5, 6, 23,
    25, 177, 179

L

Lord's Supper, 97, 104
Luther, Martin, 9, 10

M

Massachusetts Bay Colony, 12
Mullins, E. Y, 168
Mullins, E.Y., 163, 164, 165,
    166, 167, 168, 169, 171,
    178
Munster rebellion, 32

N

New England, 5, 7, 10, 12, 13,
    19, 21, 27, 40, 77, 78, 179
New England colonies, 5, 6
New Model Army, 40, 44, 52,
    157
Ninety Five Theses, 9
Non-Conformists, 13, 144, 150
Norcott, John, 128

O

Old Covenant, 84, 85, 95, 113,
    136
Open-communion, 59
Open-membership, 60
Owen, John, 41, 42, 43, 151,
    170, 178, 179
Oxford, 19

P

Parliament, 24, 29, 32, 39, 40,
    41, 42, 43, 68, 144, 151,
    157, 170

Patience, Sarah
  death, 20
Patient, Sarah, 20, 146
  death, 149
Patient, Thomas
  Army chaplain, 3, 50, 54
  Calvinist, 34, 77
  Congregationalist, 7
  Conversion, 77
  Cromwellian army, 19
  Death, 5, 20, 147
  Elder, 148
  Family, 6, 19, 20, 21
  Ireland, 50
  Irish ministry, 39
  Kent Evangelistic Tour, 35
  Marriage, 20
  On Baptism, iii, ii, 1, 2, 5, 34, 66, 75, 108, 120, 124, 125, 126, 127, 132, 159, 160, 162
  Paedobaptist, 7, 13, 14
  Persecution, 14, 34, 78
  Trade, 6
Pentecost, 79
Pilgrims, 12
Pithay Baptist Church, ii, 143
Plymouth Colony, 12
Pope, 9, 39, 40
Presbyterians, 11, 31, 120
Protectorate, ii, 26, 69, 70, 71, 72
Protestants, 9, 10, 44, 174
Puritan, iv, 1, 3, 6, 8, 10, 11, 12, 14, 19, 41, 42, 44, 50, 64, 77, 147, 152

Q

Queen Elizabeth I, 9

R

Reformation, 1, 8, 9, 39, 151
Reformers, 9, 152
Regeneration, 97, 104, 107
Religious Liberty, 3, 162
Renaissance, 9
Rogers, John, 47, 55, 56, 59, 60, 61, 65, 153, 178
Roman Catholic, 9
Royalists, 44, 45

S

Sanctification, 30, 104, 135, 136, 139
Sankey, Jerome, 62
Scotland, 23, 40, 178
Separatist, 12–16, 22, 27, 28, 155
Soteriology, 2, 10
Spilsbury, John, 22, 23
Stevens, Anne, 36

T

The Corporation Act, 144
Total depravity, 90
Trinity, 43, 65, 81, 111
Trinity College, 108
Typology, 96

U

Universalism, 98

W

Warren, Edward Sr, 108
Warren, Edward Jr., 108, 109
Waterford, ii, 45, 52, 54, 55, 56, 57, 60, 63, 180
Wexford, 44, 45, 52
Williams, Roger, 78, 166, 168, 170, 180
Winter, Samuel, 65
Woodman, Nicolas, 36

Scripture Index

Old Testament

Genesis		2 Chronicles	
17:7	113	26:14–15	86
17:8	113	Proverbs	
17:9	94	18:22	2
Leviticus		Ezekiel	
20:21	8	14:1–5	86

New Testament

Matthew	
3:6	152
16:18	48
18:17	119
19:13–15	83
21:43	102
28:18	94
28:19	94
28:19–20	49, 109
29:19	68
18:	30

Mark	
7:7	86

John	
9:4	5, 64, 92, 117

Acts	
2:39	77, 100, 105, 113
2:37–38	66
8:37	152
8:38–39	95
13:45–46	101
16:40	69
16:32–34	69

Romans	
6:4	111
9:6–8	114
11:16–17	79

1 Corinthians	
1:2	152
7:14	78, 100, 105
10:1–3	81, 101
12:13	51, 88, 152

2 Corinthians	
6:17	152
7:14	106

Galatians	
3:16	113
4:21	84, 101
4:21–31	84
5:2	112
5:6	80
6:16	80

Ephesians	
1:1	152
4:3–4	89

Philippians	
2:12–15	92
2:12–15	92

Colossians	
2:12	111

Hebrews	
8:13	80
12:1	154
12:2	154

1 Peter	
3:21	95

Name	Date Read

H&E Publishing

WWW.HESEDANDEMET.COM

www.ingramcontent.com/pod-product-compliance
Lightning Source LLC
Chambersburg PA
CBHW020533080526
44583CB00013B/847